THE OFFICIAL **NATIONAL PARK GUIDE**

THE PEAK DISTRICT

Author and series editor Roly Smith

Photographs by Ray Manley

PEVENSEY GUIDES

The Pevensey Press is an imprint of
David & Charles

First published in the UK in 2000

Map artwork by Chartwell Illustrators

A catalogue record for this book is
available from the British Library.

ISBN 1 898630 10 0 (paperback)
ISBN 1 898630 24 0 (hardback)

Book design by
Les Dominey Design Company, Exeter
and printed in China by
Hong Kong Graphic & Printing Limited
for David & Charles
Brunel House   Newton Abbot   Devon

Contents

Page 1: The unique collection of Saxon and medieval carved stones in the south porch of the parish church of All Saints, Bakewell is evidence of the antiquity of the site

Pages 2–3: Pickering Tor, Dovedale

Left: The oak-panelled, fourteenth-century Banqueting Hall at Haddon Hall

Front cover: (top) The Salt Cellar, Derwent Edge; (below) Wolfscote Dale; (front flap) Sunset sheep, Gardom's Edge; Tissington well dressing
Back cover: (top) Magpie Mine, Sheldon; (below) millstones below Stanage Edge

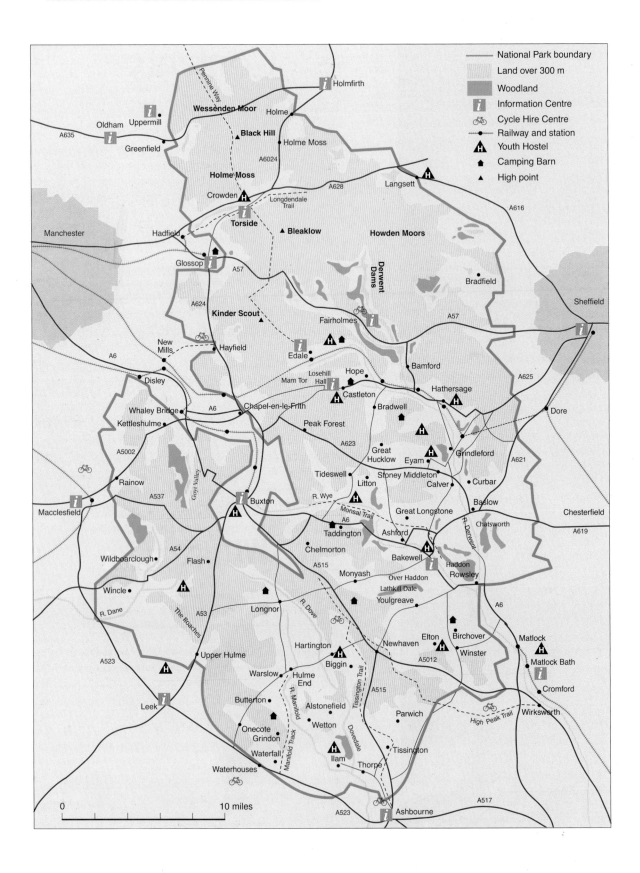

Foreword

by Professor Ian Mercer CBE, Secretary General, Association of National Park Authorities

The National Parks of Great Britain are very special places. Their landscapes include the most remote and dramatic hills and coasts in England and Wales, as well as the wild wetlands of the Broads. They still support the farming communities which have fashioned their detail over the centuries. They form the highest rank of the protected areas which society put in place in 1949. So, 1999 saw the fiftieth anniversary of the founding legislation which, incidentally, provided for Areas of Outstanding Natural Beauty, Nature Reserves, Areas of Special Scientific Interest and Long Distance Footpaths, as well as for National Parks.

In the eight years following that, ten Parks were designated. The Lake District, the Peak, Snowdonia and Dartmoor were already well visited, as were the North York Moors, Pembrokeshire Coast, Yorkshire Dales and Exmoor which quickly followed. The Brecon Beacons and Northumberland had their devotees too, though perhaps in lesser numbers then. The special quality of each of these places was already well known, and while those involved may not have predicted the numbers, mobility or aspirations of visitors accurately, the foresight of the landscape protection system cannot be too highly praised.

That system has had to evolve – not just to accommodate visitor numbers, but to meet the pressures flowing from agricultural change, hunger for housing and roadstone, thirst for water, and military manoeuvring – and indeed, the Norfolk and Suffolk Broads were added to the list in 1989. National Parks are now cared for by free-standing authorities who control development, hold land, grant-aid farmers and others, provide wardens, information, car parks and loos, clear footpaths and litter, plant trees and partner many other agents in pursuit of the purposes for which National Parks exist. Those purposes are paramount for all public agencies' consideration when they act within the Parks. They are:

- the conservation of the natural beauty, wildlife and cultural heritage of the area, and
- the promotion of the understanding and enjoyment of its special qualities by the public.

The National Park Authorities must, in pursuing those purposes, foster social and economic well-being. They now bring in some £48 million a year between them to be deployed in the Parks, in addition to normal local public spending.

This book is first a celebration of the National Park, of all its special qualities and of the people whose predecessors produced and maintained the detail of its character. The series to which this book belongs celebrates too the first fifty years of National Park protection in the United Kingdom, the foresight of the founding fathers, and the contributions since of individuals like John Sandford, Reg Hookway and Ron Edwards. The book and the series also mark the work of the present National Park Authorities and their staff, at the beginning of the next fifty years, and of the third millennium of historic time. Their dedication to their Parks is only matched by their aspiration for the sustainable enhancement of the living landscapes for which they are responsible. They need, and hope for, your support.

In the new century, national assets will only be properly maintained if the national will to conserve them is made manifest to national governments. I hope this book will whet your appetite for the National Park, or help you get more from your visit, and provoke you to use your democratic influence on its behalf. In any case it will remind you of the glories of one of the jewels in Britain's landscape crown. Do enjoy it.

Introducing the Peak District

Travelling across the vast, empty expanse of the Eastern Moors of the Peak District at night can quite literally be an enlightening experience. The barren, windswept acres of Big Moor, Hallam Moor and Beeley Moor have not changed much since the Bronze Age when, as recent discoveries have shown, a sizeable population of farmers scratched a living from these now-uninhabited heights.

Those first farmers of up to 4,000 years ago knew the same pitch blackness of the moorland night, lit only by the stars above on which they may have aligned some of their ritual monuments of monolithic standing stones and circles, which still rise enigmatically from the rank moorgrass and heather.

But as the modern traveller makes his way eastwards, a garish orange glow lights the night sky ahead, masking out the stars. And as he reaches the edge of the moor and starts the long descent into the plain on one of the many, ruler-straight Enclosure Act roads, there spread out below him like a field of fallen stars twinkle the street lights of some of the biggest industrial conurbations of northern Britain.

Opposite: Land of the bogtrotter. The approach to Kinder Scout and original start of the Pennine Way in Grindsbrook, Edale

Below: A rainbow lights the White Peak landscape below Longstone Edge

*Above: A typical Dark Peak clough –
Holme Clough which runs off Black
Hill
Opposite: Waterfalls in the Fair
Brook, on the northern approach to
Kinder Scout*

The contrast could not be more striking, and has been the excuse for generations of guidebook authors to use the cliché that the Peak District is an 'inland island' of unspoilt greenery set in a sea of industrialisation. This impression was reinforced even more graphically by more recent night-time satellite photographs of Britain, where the actual outline of the Peak District National Park boundary can be picked out precisely as an island of darkness hemmed in by the glowing street lights of the neighbouring cities (*see illustration on left*).

History shows that the Peak has always been a place apart from the rest of northern Britain. Its earliest known named inhabitants were the Saxon *Pecsaetan* – the 'people of the Peak' – a separate and independent tribe from the surrounding Mercians who ruled much of central England during the so-called Dark Ages. And there were, and some would say still are, pockets of Celtic culture and religion here long after Christianity had been adopted by the rest of the country. This apartness is echoed in the many strange and often unique ancient customs and legends which have lived on in these limestone and gritstone hills while they have disappeared and been long forgotten elsewhere in Britain. Examples of this are the ancient, originally pagan custom of well dressing, and the mysterious Castleton Garlanding Ceremony, which perhaps was a celebration of the rebirth of spring.

DARK AND WHITE

There are two, quite distinct types of scenery in the Peak District – endowing the landscape with characteristics which have sometimes been described as equating to male and female. These contrasting yet complimentary types of scenery have over the years been summarised to the Dark Peak and the White Peak, abbreviations

Above: Sheep graze safely among the intricate network of drystone walls, near Wardlow

Opposite: Looking down into Upperdale and the deeply incised valley of the River Wye from Monsal Head. The line of the former Midland Railway, now the Monsal Trail, can be seen on the left

which have been adopted by the Ordnance Survey for their popular Outdoor Leisure maps.

The name of the Dark Peak aptly describes the stern, masculine nature of the northern, eastern and western moorlands of the Peak District. This is a land of dark, brooding tablelands which are punctuated by steep, rocky valleys known as cloughs; exotic, wind-carved tors, and bordered by abrupt, precipituous walls of naked rock, known here as 'edges'.

The moors are dominated by heather, bilberry and moorgrass but the highest points, such as Kinder Scout, Bleaklow and Black Hill, which constitute the largest area of land in England above 2,000ft (610m), have been described as examples of 'land at the end of its tether'. Here, years of over-grazing, acid rain and natural erosion has robbed the soil of any vegetation at all, and dark and dank peat bogs abound. These vast areas of bare peat are dissected by deep natural drainage channels called groughs (pronounced 'gruffs'), bordered by banks of peat which are known as hags. The Dark Peak moors are founded on a deep layer of impermeable grey millstone grit sandstones which do not allow the easy drainage of water and are the main reason for the peat forming into those evil bogs.

This forbidding land, which marks the start of the 270-mile (435km) Pennine Way, offers some of the most challenging and difficult walking in the whole of Britain, and its aficionados are known by the entirely descriptive name of 'bogtrotters'.

The relationship between the Dark Peak and White Peak is perhaps best described by imagining the balding pate of a man. The remaining 'hair' can be seen as the Dark Peak moors to the north, east and west, leaving the exposed 'skin' of the central limestone plateau of the White Peak exposed in the middle and south.

Although they were both formed during the same Carboniferous period around 350 million years ago, the pearly-white limestone represents the skeleton of the Peak District landscape and is the older of the two distinctive rock types. It therefore lies below the gritstone moors and edges but has been exposed by aeons of uplifting and erosion to create the 1,000ft (300m) central limestone plateau which is dissected by its distinctive, steep-sided dales, and known as the White Peak.

This is altogether a more gentle, feminine kind of landscape than the Dark Peak, where the seductive, swelling contours of the plateau are bound together by mile after mile of an intricate network of drystone walls. This is the feature of the Peak District which often makes the most lasting impression on the first-time visitor, especially those coming from the hedged and wooded landscapes of the south. It has been estimated that there are 26,000 miles of drystone walls in the White Peak alone, and the Farm and Countryside Service of the National Park Authority gives grants to maintain the most important of these historically and visually important land boundaries.

The Palace of the Peak – Chatsworth, Derbyshire home of the Dukes of Devonshire, glows in the sun seen from across the River Derwent

John Ruskin, the nineteenth-century critic and conservationist, wrote: 'The whole gift of the country is in its glens. The wide acreage of field or moor above is wholly without interest; it is only in the clefts of it, and the dingles, that the traveller finds his joy'. While that may be too much of a generalisation today – the most important prehistoric remains, like the stone circle and henge of Arbor Low for example, are found high on the limestone plateau – most people still love the dales of the White Peak. Unlike those of the Yorkshire Dales further north in the Pennines, most of the Derbyshire and Staffordshire dales of the Peak District are too narrow to have a road running through them. Therefore they are almost exclusively the preserve of the walker, who come in their thousands to enjoy the scenic splendour of places like Dovedale, Monsal Dale and Lathkill Dale.

This popularity inevitably brings problems for the National Park Authority in its wake, and footpaths in places like Dovedale are in need of almost constant restoration through overuse and consquent erosion. The Stepping Stones at the entrance to Dovedale are best avoided in the middle of summer, and in any case, the best time to appreciate the stunning rock architecture of the dales is in the winter when the leaves are off the trees.

The Peak District dales are also the showplaces for Peak District wildlife, and most of the best are incorporated into the Derbyshire Dales National Nature Reserve, or protected as Sites of Special Scientific Interest (SSSIs), Special Areas of Conservation (SACs), or Environmentally Sensitive Areas (ESAs).

Lying as a kind of transition zone, or the jam in the sandwich, between the gritstone moors of the Dark Peak and the limestone plateau and dales of the White Peak; broad, well-wooded and fertile shale valleys carry the Peak's major rivers, such as the Derwent and the Wye. Here is where many of the major settlements lie, and where the landed gentry built the famous stately homes of the Peak, such as the Duke of Devonshire's Chatsworth and the Duke of Rutland's Haddon Hall, near Bakewell.

AT THE CROSSROADS

The Peak District stands at the crossroads of Britain – on the boundary between the highland and lowland zones and showing aspects of both.

This is noticeable first in the scenery, where the hedged cornfields and well-wooded landscapes of the Midlands and south give way to open, stony pastures enclosed by those miles of patiently-constructed drystone walls.

The change is also noticeable in vegetation and wildlife. The Peak marks the northern boundary of a number of lowland plants and animals, such as the ivy-leaved bell-flower, the stemless thistle and the nuthatch. But it is also on the southern boundary of northern species such as the cowberry and bearberry, the globe flower, the bird cherry, mossy saxifrage and melancholy thistle, as well as the reintroduced mountain or blue hare, which is once again common on the eastern and northern moors.

North of that invisible border, human settlements change also. Villages and hamlets are often small and isolated, sometimes no more than a couple of farmsteads sheltering behind a belt of ash or sycamore in a hollow. And the buildings are, of course, no longer built of brick but of the locally abundant stone, seeming to grow almost organically from the rocky soil which gave them birth. White Peak and Dark Peak villages are built of limestone or gritstone respectively, marking that fundamental geological divide in their stonework which can also be sometimes seen in the same length of a drystone wall.

The biggest town and natural 'capital' of the Peak District is Bakewell, with a population of only 4,000 people. The total population of the National Park is 38,000.

These Peaklanders, or Peakrills as they were once known, are undoubtedly of North Country stock, and their attitudes are generally harder and more uncompromising. They like their own company and use short, blunt words compared with the long-winded and more gregarious southerners. Their attitude to religion is different too, and non-conformism, particularly Methodism, is still strong in Peakland villages, where the chapel is often the centre of community life.

Overleaf: One of the Peak's few peaks deserving the name, distant Shutlingsloe dominates the snow-covered Cheshire moors in this view from below Shining Tor

Below: An ancient, low-parapeted packhorse bridge crosses the River Bradford near Youlgreave, one of many to be found in the area

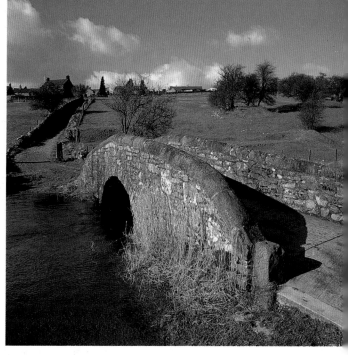

PEAK PARADOXES

The Peak District is an area full of contradictions. Despite the name, there are only a handful of hills which justify the name 'peak', including Shutlingsloe on the western fringe; Chrome and Parkhouse Hills in the Upper Dove, and Lose Hill in the Hope Valley. The name comes from the Old English *peac* which meant any sort of knoll or hill, and did not then have Dr Johnson's meaning of 'a sharply pointed summit'.

Many people come to the Peak District looking for a snow-capped Matterhorn and go away disappointed – the abiding perspective in the Peak is nearly always of a horizontal tableland. This is especially true of the region's highest point of Kinder Scout, 2,088ft (636m), which is still misleadingly marked on some modern maps as 'The Peak'. The Peak is a district, not a mountain, and has been known as such since the days of Michael Drayton in the sixteenth century. In any case, anywhere less like a 'sharply pointed summit' would be hard to imagine than this 7-square-mile morass of peat groughs and hags.

Another Peakland paradox is the name 'low' which is so common on the Peak District map. There are estimated to be no fewer than seventy of these in the White Peak alone, and almost without exception, they mark a hill or a high point in the landscape.

The confusing name again comes from the Old English, *hlaw*, which meant a burial mound or hill, usually a tumulus dating from the Bronze Age. So in other words, where you see 'low' in the Peak District, it usually denotes a high place. Then of course, just to confuse the issue even further, there is the delightfully paradoxical 'High Low' on the hills above Hathersage in the Hope Valley.

FIRST AND LAST

The Peak District became the first National Park in Britain when its designation was confirmed by the post-War Labour Government on 17 April, 1951. In many important respects, it was a National Park where it was most needed.

The Hope Valley Cement Works, seen here from above Pindale, is an important local provider of jobs

As already described, the Peak District stood out as the last unspoilt open space between Manchester and Sheffield and the rest of the great conurbations of northern and central England. The populations of those teeming cities had long used the Peak for their weekend recreation, but there were thorny and unresolved problems of access to the high northern moors, which were at that time strictly preserved for grouse shooting. This pressure for access culminated in the famous 'Battle of Kinder Scout' in April 1932, when a well-publicised mass trespass on the western slopes of the Peak's reigning summit had resulted in five of the ringleaders being jailed for 'riotous assembly'.

At this time, the suburbia, roadside signs and the red-brick villas of these fast-expanding cities were insidiously creeping out towards the green hills of the Peak, unchecked and unopposed by any planning authority. There were plans for steel works in Edale, and even for a Grand Prix motor racing circuit around the glorious White Peak countryside north of Hartington. Groups like the Standing Committee on National Parks and the Sheffield and Peak branch of the Council for the Preservation of Rural England fought off some of these threats, but it was obvious that legislation was urgently needed.

It eventually came with the passing of the 1949 National Parks and Access to the Countryside Act, which resulted from the recommendations of John Dower's seminal report on the need for National Parks in Britain which was published in 1945. Dower had considered that 'the ever-spreading inferno' of limestone quarries and lime-works near Buxton was the worst disfigurement of the Peak District, and Sir Arthur Hobhouse's Report two years later, which recommended the Peak as one of the first Parks, stated: 'There is no other area which has evoked more strenuous public effort to safeguard its beauty. Its very proximity to the industrial towns renders it as vulnerable as it is valuable.'

The problem of quarrying has still not gone away. There are still seventy quarry sites within the National Park, of which fifty are registered as active.

A startling portrayal of the proximity of urban sprawl to the moorlands of the Peak: the tower blocks of Sheffield as seen from the Eastern Moors within the National Park

But Hobhouse added that the controversy over access to uncultivated moorland reached its height in the Peak District, where 'an altercation with a gamekeeper may often mar a day's serenity'. His conclusion was: 'A national park in the Peak District will not justify its name unless this problem is satisfactorily solved.'

The new Peak District National Park Authority acted swiftly to negotiate access agreements with many of the largest moorland owners in the Dark Peak, and today over 80 square miles (207 sq km) of the 555-square-mile (1,438 sq km) National Park are open for walkers to roam at will, subject to closure on shooting days and a common-sense set of by-laws. Today, over 60 per cent of access agreements in Britain are in the Peak District, and the Labour Government's promise of open access to mountain and moorland will effectively double the open access area that the Park Authority will have to manage for visitors.

The proximity to the huge populations of the Midlands and north – half the population of England lives within 60 miles of the Peak District (more than within 60 miles of Charing Cross) – has inevitably led to problems of congestion at peak times. It has been claimed that the 22 million day visits to the Peak District National Park make it the second most visited National Park in the world, and the narrow Peakland roads and paths often show signs of serious congestion and wear and tear.

'Green' tourism is the buzz word at the moment, and through its support of public transport initiatives and multiple benefit schemes such as the network of 'camping barns', the Park Authority is leading the way in sustainable development. Working in partnership with other agencies and the local communities, the authority is forging new links where the enormous task of caring for this fragile landscape can be shared and 'owned' by others.

The enormous challenge facing the newly reconstituted Peak District National Park Authority is to continue to safeguard and protect this precious unspoilt island so that future generations can continue to enjoy its unique qualities as much as we do today.

1 The rocks beneath: geology and scenery

Opposite: Ilam Rock in Dovedale is a splendid example of the natural architectural feature which can be created by the differential erosion of reef limestone

Below: The bedding planes in successive layers of limestone are clearly seen in Parson's Tor in Upper Lathkill Dale

Picture the scene. You are floating in the middle of a broad, shallow tropical lagoon where the only sound is the gentle sigh of the great rollers as they break rhythmically over a distant coral reef, which can just be seen shimmering like a mirage on the horizon.

The temperature is sizzling into the 90s and the sun beats down with a ferocious, eye-blinking intensity, for you are only a few degrees south of the Equator. As the sun reflects off the translucent water of the lagoon, you occasionally get glimpses of the bottom, where tangled forests of sea lilies wave their feathery arms in unison with the constantly shifting currents. If you had an aqua-lung, you could dive beneath the clear blue waters and see strange-looking shellfish darting across the lagoon bottom, weaving in and out of the lily forests and waving their tentacles in constant search of sustenance. As they die, the lime-rich bodies of these and countless other microscopic sea creatures float gently to the bottom, gradually building up enormous deposits of skeletal debris.

Out on those distant fringing reefs, banks of seaweeds undulate to a different, stronger rhythm, dictated by the greater open ocean beyond. And in their waving branches, they catch those fine particles of lime from the water and build up huge, mound-like masses which eventually rise above the level of the sea. Great rollers crash in on these upstanding reefs, sending white, foaming spray flying up into the clear blue air.

Beneath the surface, brachiopods, goniatites and small, mussel-like creatures scuttle about as they seek shelter and food among the seaweed forests and further large colonies of sea-lilies.

Then without warning, the peace of the tropical lagoon is shattered by an enormous underwater rumbling. The still waters of the lagoon start to boil and foam as the floor erupts in a cloud of steam and falling ash particles. The world darkens as the sun is blotted out by huge clouds of steam vapour and falling ash, as the tropical Paradise of a few minutes ago is transformed into a fiery, volcanic Hell.

The eruption does not last long, but it is long enough to cover part of the sea bed with a sheet of viscous larva which cools rapidly in contact with the sea water and hardens to form a dark blanket over the limestones. Peace soon returns again to our tropical lagoon, and that violent volcanic incident is forgotten as if nothing had happened. All evidence of it is soon buried under that perpetual underwater drizzle of dead and dying sea creatures.

To witness such primordial scenes, you might be excused for thinking that you had somehow strayed thousands of miles to the south to a South Pacific atoll – Bikini or Tahiti perhaps – where such scenes are commonplace. But no, you were actually closer to the sites of modern-day Ballidon or Tideswell, and you had been magically transported back in time to between 325 and 360 million years ago. What we now know as the Peak District was then situated 5 to 10 degrees south of the Equator, as opposed to over 50 degrees to the north of it as it is today.

And what you were watching as you floated serenely on that deceptively peaceful tropical lagoon was the Genesis of what we now know as the White Peak – the limestone skeleton of the Peak District, and the oldest of the rocks still visible in the area. At the time, what we now know as the White Peak lay at the centre of a huge tropical lagoon some 25 miles long from north to south from modern Wirksworth to Castleton, and 10 miles wide, between what is now Bakewell and Buxton.

When that imaginary time machine whisked you back to the period known to geologists as the Carboniferous, you witnessed one of the many cataclysmic interludes which have created the landscape known and loved by millions today. And those links with the incredibly ancient past can still be seen everywhere in the limestones of the White Peak, if you know what to look for. It is perhaps hard to equate that blissful tropical scene and climate with that of today as you battle your way through a winter blizzard across the White Peak plateau.

Elsewhere, the regular horizontal joints in the crags of some of the dales sides, such those that can be seen in Stoney Middleton Dale, Lathkill Dale, Miller's Dale and Chee Dale, show the so-called bedding planes of the various stages of the deposition of those microscopic sea creatures in the calm centre of that clear, still lagoon. Today, they form convenient ledges for nesting kestrels or crows, and resting places and belay points for intrepid rock climbers.

Some appreciation of the immensity of the time scale of the 35 million years of this geological epoch can be gauged when it is realised that the overall thickness of the White Peak's limestone has been measured at over 2,000ft (or 600m).

Fossilised crinoids stand out in sharp relief in this White Peak gatepost

DERBYSHIRE SCREWS

As you stop to shelter from the biting wind in the lee of a drystone wall on the White Peak plateau, you might just notice the gatepost or squeezer stile you are leaning against contains the unmistakable fossil remains of long-dead, land-building sea creatures of 350 million years ago, now polished by the brushing of generations of cattle and walkers.

Those strange, segmented stone stalks, known locally as 'Derbyshire screws' because of their uncanny resemblance to a screw thread, are the remains of ancient sea lilies. Known as crinoids, they were actually not plants at all but primitive sea animals, most closely related to our present day starfish. In that tropical Paradise, they grew up to 10ft in height with five branching arms which spread like the fronds of a palm tree from the central 'trunk'.

In places like disused Ricklow Quarry at the head of Lathkill Dale, these crinoidal limestones were quarried, cut and polished for use as ornamental stone. The sections and cross-sections of the crinoids create attractive and random patterns or 'figures' when cut, which show up white against a light grey background when polished. They were much prized in Victorian times, and examples can be seen in the polished floors of Chatsworth House and other stately homes, and more recently in the floor of the nave of the rebuilt Cathedral of St Michael in Coventry.

The majority of the White Peak plateau, an area of rolling pastureland enmeshed by a network of the distinctive drystone walls and seldom falling below the 1,000ft (300m) contour, was laid down during these calm and settled conditions. And the purity and availability of that limestone has littered the edges of the plateau with some of the largest quarries in Europe – so big they are visible by satellites from space.

And what of those fringing reefs which bordered that broad, peaceful lagoon? Today's visitor to the Peak District National Park who appreciates the rugged scenery of the dales has cause to thank those coral-forming creatures of so many millions of years ago. They created some of the most outstanding landscape features of the White Peak – including some of the Peak's only real peaks.

A walk in Dovedale – perhaps the most famous dale of all thanks to early publicity by anglers Izaak Walton and Charles Cotton – passes a whole collection of fancifully-named rock features, all of which were formed by the erosion-resistant qualities of these reef limestones. The shapely twin southern sentinels of Bunster Hill and Thorpe Cloud are the first examples, but they are followed in swift succession by features like the Twelve Apostles, Lover's Leap, Tissington Spires, Ilam Rock and Pickering Tor, more easily seen today thanks to the National Trust's tree-clearance policies. And where the rushing Dove, swollen and made even more abrasive by the meltwater of Ice Age glaciers, swirled into weakness in the rock, cavernous features like the natural arch of Reynard's Cave and the great gaping maws of Dove Holes were formed.

Elsewhere, those ancient marginal reefs formed other upstanding features like Thor's Cave and crag, Beeston Tor and Ecton Hill in the neighbouring Manifold Valley; High Tor at Matlock; and around Castleton in the dramatic pass of The Winnats, Cave Dale and the soaring entrance gorge to Peak Cavern.

The great circular hollows of Dove Holes in Dovedale were caused by the swirling power of the meltwater from Ice Age glaciers 10,000 years ago

The same volcanic heat and the mineral reactions caused by enormous pressure built up under the incredible depths of sediments created yet another kind of limestone which occurs in certain southern pockets of the White Peak. This porous, fawn or dun coloured rock is known as dolomitic limestone – after the mountain range in the Italian Alps. It is found outcropping along the B5056 Grangemill-Ballidon road and more famously around the popular rock climbing crags of Harborough and Rainster Rocks, just outside the Park boundary near Brassington.

The viscous lavas which spewed forth from their underwater birthplace during that brief volcanic interlude we witnessed earlier also weathered differently from the main mass of limestone. They can be seen as darker, brown rocks – known to lead miners as 'toadstones' – at places like Black Rock Corner, on the A6 between Bakewell and Buxton, and even more spectacularly in Tideswell Dale, where a bed of clay overlaid by the lava was baked by its heat and solidified into hexagonal columns just like the more famous basalts of the Giant's Causeway in County Antrim or on the Hebridean island of Staffa. Much of the mineral wealth of the Peak – particularly the lead mining industry which has been so important in the economic history of the White Peak since Roman times – also had its birth at this time. As scalding, salty solutions were forced up through and filled the many cracks and fissures in the limestone, they eventually cooled and crystallised into veins of galena (lead), fluorspar, baryte and calcite. On the south-western side of the Park in the upper Manifold Valley, the solutions seem to have been composed differently and may have come from a different origin, for at Ecton Hill, the crystallised minerals are not lead but copper-based. The mineral rights to the incredibly pure and rich copper 'pipe' at Ecton were owned by the Duke of Devonshire, and they made him a very rich man during the eighteenth century. The profits from Ecton were said to have paid for the 5th Duke's stylish expansion of the town of Buxton into a fashionable spa, and included the building of the famous Crescent and Great Stables and Riding School, now the Devonshire Royal Hospital.

Fluorspar is still commercially mined in the Peak District, where it is a source of the flouride used in water and toothpaste, and barytes is still used a filler in paper and paint manufacture. Perhaps the most famous Peak District fluorspar, however, is Blue John, a beautiful, delicately-banded semi-precious stone found only in the Treak Cliff and Winnats Pass area, near Castleton. It is thought to have got its name from the French *bleu-jaune* ('blue-yellow'), descriptive of some of the colours of the translucent bands which characterise it.

But without doubt the single most important mineral industry in the White Peak has been that of the extraction of lead. The discovery of massive Roman 'pigs' of lead all over the country inscribed with the name of *Lutudarum* – a site which has still to be conclusively identified but certainly referred to the Peak District – shows that it began nearly 2,000 years ago. The Romans were probably able to mine lead from surface deposits to line their sophisticated plumbing systems and baths. Odin Mine, near Castleton, is often claimed to be the earliest identifiable lead mine, perhaps because of its dedication to the Norse god of death, magic and madness.

The heyday of the White Peak's lead mining industry was during the eighteenth century, when at least 10,000 miners were at work in about 30,000 workings in the White Peak. Most were not full-time miners, but combined their underground delvings with farming in a dual economy which until recently, was still widely practised with the quarrying of limestone replacing lead mining.

Almost every pasture field you look at on the White Peak plateau will be pitted and pock-marked with the humps and hollows of the workings of 't'owd man', as

The spectacular gorge of the Winnats Pass near Castleton is thought to have been formed as an inter-reef channel in Carboniferous times, later re-excavated by glacial meltwater

TWIN PEAKS

Perhaps the most startling examples of the differential erosion of reef limestones can be found in the quieter stretches of the Upper Dove, far from the madding crowds which always seem to be queuing to cross the famous Stepping Stones, and nearer to the source of the River on Axe Edge. Here the sharply pointed summits and knife-edge ridges of Chrome and Parkhouse Hills, above Hollinsclough, can take on the appearance of real Alpine giants, especially after a snowfall. Viewed from the tiny hamlet of Crowdicote on the Monyash-Longnor road, they dominate the northern end of the dale with a fair impression of real mountains. In truth, these are the only hills that can, with any justification, be called peaks in the whole of the Peak District.

Chrome (left) and Parkhouse Hills dominate the Upper Dove Valley, near Crowdecote. They are further examples of harder, reef limestone knolls which have withstood the forces of erosion to leave some of the few sharply pointed peaks in the Peak District

The reconstructed horse gin at Magpie Mine, near Sheldon

Alternating beds of occasionally oil-bearing shale and shale-grit are prominently exposed in the banks of the River Noe

the spirit and presence of the old lead miners are known today. The long lines of lead 'rakes' – the major source of large qualities of lead ore deposited vertically between two walls of rock and extending, in some cases, for miles across the countryside – can still be traced either by their sheltering belts of trees, designed to keep cattle away, or by the deep vertical shafts which plunge down for hundreds of feet.

The best-preserved and most complete example of a White Peak lead mine is Magpie Mine, high on the plateau near Sheldon. These evocative ruins, including a square, Derbyshire-built pumping house chimney and a round Cornish-built one, stand over 700ft (200m) deep shafts which were worked more or less continuously for over 200 years. The last attempt to win the precious ore from Magpie is marked by the black winding gear and rusting, corrugated iron sheds dating from the 1950s, and now protected like the rest of the buildings as an ancient monument. Magpie Mine is now used as a field study centre by the Peak District Mines Historical Society.

THE DARK PEAK

It's time for us to climb back into our time machine for the next episode in the long geological history of the Peak District. Later in that warm, tropical Carboniferous period, the broad shallow lagoon which was the basis of the limestone White Peak started to be invaded by a more subtle, quieter influence than the volcanoes of the past. Huge deltas of mud and silt were gradually deposited by gigantic rivers flowing down from the north, from higher ground in what we now know as Scotland.

Conditions on these vast, swampy deltas would have been identical to those existing on the Mississippi, Nile or Ganges of today. Vast qualities of sand and silt were carried down from the fast-eroding northern mountains and spread in braided channels and thick, constantly-shifting sand banks which ebbed and flowed across the shallow lagoon.

Sometimes the deposits were gritty sands, which were eventually to give us the massive millstone grit sandstones of the Eastern Edges, The Roaches, Kinder Scout and Bleaklow. At other times, thinner muds and silts dominated, giving us the unstable, thin shaley layers so well exposed in the 'shivering' eastern face of Mam Tor at the head of the Hope Valley. These dark, alternating layers of shale, siltstones and sandstones (which are usually abbreviated to gritstone in the Peak), have been given the generic name of the Dark Peak, to differentiate them from the pearly-grey of the limestone White Peak.

Where the land was allowed to build up, the invading vegetation was luxuriant. Scale-barked, tropical rain forest-type trees towered above the swamp, with thick, dripping mosses hanging from their boughs, and huge, tree-sized ferns thriving in the wet, moist conditions beneath. It would have been a scene reminiscent of the present day Amazonian jungle – again a scene hard to imagine as you stand on an airy gritstone edge today.

Later deposits formed from the remains of this lush, tropical forest created the

Top: The 'shivering' mountain: Mam Tor
Above: The massively bedded Chatsworth Grits are exposed in the face of Froggatt Edge above the Derwent Valley, a popular venue for rock-climbing

Opposite: The serrated skyline of Ramshaw Rocks, which overhang the Buxton–Leek road, are a series of wind and frost-eroded tors formed from the erosion-resistant millstone grit

Below: Noe Stool, which takes its name from the main river in the Edale valley, is a prominent feature on the southern edge of Kinder Scout. It is a typical, anvil-shaped tor formed from millstone grit

Above: Mother Cap: a gritstone tor above Millstone Edge overlooking the Hope Valley

coal measures which still exist to the east of the Peak District in the North East Derbyshire coalfield. They gave us the name of the period (Carboniferous = coal bearing). There are a few thin coal seams in the Peak District, notably in the Upper Goyt Valley and in the bowl of Goldsitch Moss east of The Roaches in Staffordshire, but most of these softer deposits have been eroded away.

And that was the fate of most of that gritstone and shale which once covered the whole of the bleached white limestone 'skeleton' of the White Peak. Aeons of uplift, erosion and weathering gradually wore away the gritstone and shale cover, leaving the limestone exposed in the centre and south of the Peak District. Today the Dark Peak exists as an upturned horseshoe enclosing the White Peak to the north, west and east.

Among the most characteristic landforms of the Dark Peak are the distinctive gritstone 'edges' which mark the boundary of the moorlands to the north, east and west. They frown down in an almost unbroken wall on the shale river valley of the Derwent to the east, and create the more broken, folded faces of The Roaches, Ramshaw Rocks and Hen Cloud in the west. The short, steep westward-facing escarpments of Derwent, Bamford, Stanage, Froggatt and Curbar are a cross-section of the remains of that former gritstone cap. Today their coarse, abrasive faces give some of the finest rock-climbing in Britain, and a promenade along their tops makes a wonderful walk. The same can be said of the Staffordshire Roaches, and the gritstone crags which rim Kinder Scout, especially around Grindsbrook and Kinder Downfall.

A characteristic feature of the Dark Peak are the weirdly-shaped, bulbous 'tors' – an Old English word which simply means a rock, rocky outcrop or hill – which stand back from so many of the Dark Peak edges. Good examples can be found on Derwent Edge, such as the Salt Cellar and the Coach and Horses or Wheel Stones; around the perimeter of Kinder Scout, such as the Woolpacks, the Pagoda and Noe Stool; and on Bleaklow, with the Trident and the Wain Stones.

These gritstone tors were formed in much the same way as those carved in granite on Dartmoor and the Cairngorms, and consist of the wind, frost and rain-eroded stumps of slightly more resistant grits formed under the surface and now upstanding after the softer surrounding rocks has been rotted and eroded away.

You don't have to be a geologist to notice the difference between the 'Twin Peaks' – Dark and White – on the ground. Apart from the obvious difference in the colour of the exposed rocks (and if there are no rocks visible, you'll see it in the stones in the drystone walls in each area), the altitude and vegetation are the main clues. The great gritstone mass of Kinder Scout, Bleaklow and Black Hill in the north of the National Park, averages 2,000ft (600m) above the sea – about twice the height of the White Peak plateau. This creates much harsher conditions and a rainfall which averages 60in (150cm) a year. The gritstone is much more massive and impervious than the limestone, so any water which falls on these high and wild plateaux tends to stay on the surface creating the build up of sphagnum moss and eventually blanket bog conditions. In drier times, this high

Sunlight catches the tottering ramparts of The Tower at Alport Castles in Alport Dale on the southern slopes of Bleaklow, said to be the largest landslip in Britain

ground was covered in trees like oak, birch and hazel, the boles of which can still sometimes be seen poking out of the groughs (drainage channels) in the blanket peat. But the inexorable build up of mosses in the saturated conditions which predominated, the 'slash-and-burn' agricultural policies of early Man, and the introduction of vast flocks of grazing sheep slowly created the vast, treeless 'wilderness' which are the Dark Peak moorlands, so beloved of the 'bogtrotters' of today.

THE FINAL POLISH

The aeons of deposition of grit and lime during the Carboniferous Period were followed by hot, dry periods known as the Permian and Triassic, between 280 and 195 million years ago. Like the rest of Britain, the Peak District became a Sahara-like desert of shifting sands and baking rocks, of which little or nothing now remains.

The age of the dinosaurs – the Jurassic – followed, leaving hardly a trace, when the area was again submerged for another mind-boggling 100 million years, before hot and dry conditions again held sway during the Teriary era of between two and 70 million years ago. The only trace of this last hot, dry interlude is now found in isolated pockets exposed on the White Peak plateau, such as at Friden, near Newhaven, where deposits of silica sand dating from this period were ultilised for making firebricks for steel furnaces.

But the final polish which shaped the Peak District known and loved by so many millions today was executed by the immense glaciers of successive Ice Ages during the period known as the Pleistocene. This scraped away the last of the millstone grit cover and, as the mighty northern glaciers finally melted around 10,000 years ago, great torrents of rushing meltwater carved out the distinctive dales of the White and Dark Peaks which are so popular among walkers today.

These freezing floodwaters also played an important role in the creation of the Peak's 'underground', the system of caves and caverns which underlie the limestone and caused the Victorian novellist Sir Arthur Conan Doyle to describe the countryside around Castleton as 'hollow'. 'Could you strike it with some gigantic hammer it would boom like a drum, or possibly cave in altogether,' he wrote in his short story, *The Terror of Blue John Gap*. The four show caves at Castleton show the visitor these underground wonders in safety, while potholers find their sport in 'sporting' caves such as Giant's, P8 and Nettle Pot south of Rushup Edge.

The freeze-thaw conditions of the retreating Ice Ages created massive instability in the rocks of the Peak District, especially in the thin shales and siltstones of the Dark Peak. This was the period of huge landslips, the most famous probably being the east face of Mam Tor, whose landslips continue to this day, sweeping away the former A625 Castleton to Chapel-en-le-Frith road in 1977, and giving the hill the nickname of 'the Shivering Mountain'. Other large landslips can be seen in the northern face of Back Tor, east of Mam Tor; in the hummocky ground north of Rushup Edge and around Abney Clough; at Lud's Church, in Back Forest near Gradbach, and at Peter's Stone near Cressbrook Dale in the White Peak.

But the largest landslip in the Peak – and possibly in Britain – is the romantically-named Alport Castles, on the eastern side of remote Alport Dale as it runs down from Bleaklow. Here, tottering towers of shales and grit have slipped away from the unstable face of Birchin Hat to create a tumbled ruin of rocks which could be mistaken for a man-made fortress.

As the ice sheets eventually retreated and the present warm, interglacial period began, the first modern flowers, plants and animals began to slowly colonise the hostile environment of the Peak District.

The hummocky, slumped landscape north of Rushup Edge in the Edale valley shows graphic evidence of landslipping after the last Ice Age, echoing the more famous landslip below Mam Tor to the east

Overleaf: Abney Clough, west of the Hope Valley near Hathersage, is a good example of a folded landscape which has been largely shaped by extensive landslipping in the ancient past. The high wind-catching ridge of Bole Hill on Eyam Moor above was utilised by lead-miners to smelt ore in bole furnaces

2 Climate, vegetation and wildlife

Below: Rare semi-natural woodlands at Padley Gorge

Opposite: Winter snow dusts the moors below Stanage Edge, looking west towards Win Hill in the middle distance with the high moors of Kinder Scout and Bleaklow beyond

The eighteenth-century traveller who noted after mounting the steep hill on the Buxton road out of Ashbourne that 'at the summit of the hill, it was a top coat colder' was only making an observation which many had made, before and since.

Top coats may have been exchanged for anoraks and fleeces today, but modern visitors, especially those coming from the south of England, have often been known to comment unfavourably and sometimes unfairly on the difference in temperature experienced as they enter the Peak District. I am not sure what they expect; it is, after all, hill country.

There can be no doubt left in the mind of the visitor who leaves the cobbled Market Place at Ashbourne and travels north to ascend the limestone plateau of the White Peak that they have well and truly left the lowlands behind. The soft, arable and neatly-hedgerowed landscape of the Midlands is gone, and in its place are miles and miles of drystone walls spread like a mesh across open, treeless pastures. Hidden from the motorist are the deep, incised dales, where crags of naked rock break through to the surface.

The accident of geography which placed the Peak District at the very heart of Britain has given it the nearest thing we have in this country to a continental-type climate. Here, in addition to the sudden change in altitude occasioned by its position at the southern extremity of the Pennines and at the start of highland Britain, its position at the centre of the island gives rise to mini-continental extremes of temperature and rainfall.

In the Peak District, as residents will readily confirm, it is usually windier, cloudier and frostier than in the surrounding lowlands. The sun is certainly seen less often, making the times when it does break the through the 'clag' all the more magical to those who are there to appreciate this rare and precious gift.

But the major climatic difference between the Peak and the surrounding lowlands is in precipitation, be it rain, hail or snow. In the mid-1970s, the highest areas of the Dark Peak were reckoned to have snow on at least seventy days every year, although personal experience and the effects of global warming and climatic change would probably suggest that it would be an overestimate today.

Frosts occur for 32 per cent of the time during December on these moors above 2,000ft (610m); compared with only 7 per cent of the time on the 1,000ft (305m) contour on the White Peak plateau. It has been estimated that the temperature falls below the threshold figure for plant growth (42 degrees F) as much as 90 per cent of the time during the winter months of January and February on the Dark Peak moorlands.

These moorlands have an annual rainfall of between 60–65in (150–163cm) on the high plateaux of Kinder Scout and Bleaklow. This compares with an average of 35–40in (88–100cm) on the limestone plateau of the White Peak in the south of the area, which itself is double that for the surrounding lowlands.

AT THE CROSSROADS

As has already been pointed out in the Introduction, the Peak District stands at the natural crossroads of Britain, where the lowlands rise to meet the highlands. As such, it is the natural meeting place for plants and animals which have both northern and southern distributions, and to a lesser extent, eastern and western species also.

The mountain or blue hare, a species which has been reintroduced to the Dark Peak moors, changes its coat to camouflage itself against the white of the winter snows (Mark Hamblin)

Among these northern types are semi-Arctic/Alpine plants such as the aptly-named cloudberry, with its delicate white flowers and raspberry-like fruit, which is quite common in places like Kinder Scout and Bleaklow, but which is not found further south in England. The cowberry and bearberry also fall into this category, while the spectacular globe flower – a member of the buttercup family, mossy saxifrage and melancholy thistle, are other characteristic northern species which also reach their southern limit in the limestone dales, particularly on their damper, northern-facing slopes. Bird cherry, with its small, black berries and delicate white flowers, is another 'northerner' which is found here, although it has been shown it cannot usually survive in the hotter, drier environment found on the southern-facing slopes of the dales.

Ivy-leaved bellflower, however, is an example of a flower which is concentrated in Wales and the south-west, and whose china-blue flowers although rare, manage to sustain a toe-hold in sheltered, moist spots in the southern part of the Peak District and no further north. Stemless thistle is a species common on the chalky downs of the south and east of England and is occasionally found on the warmer

*Looking down on the upper
reaches of Lathkill Dale, which
lies at the heart of English
Nature's flagship Derbyshire
Dales National Nature Reserve*

FLORAL FLAGSHIP

*In 1972, twenty-one years after
the foundation of the National
Park, parts of Lathkill Dale and
Monk's Dale were designated by
the Nature Conservancy as the
134th National Nature Reserve
to be established in Britain. The
area protected covered 158
acres (64ha), and has since
gradually been extended into
parts of Cressbrook Dale, Biggin
Dale, Long Dale, and most
recently Hay Dale, so that the
Derbyshire Dales NNR now
covers 845 acres (342ha). It is
heralded by English Nature, the
successor to the Nature
Conservancy as the Government's
wildlife watchdog as one of their
most-visited 'flagship' reserves.
Lathkill Dale alone is estimated
to receive 100,000 visitors a year
– exactly half the estimated total
which visits the entire NNR.*

and drier south-facing sides of the limestone dales. But it too damp even here to regularly set its seed and spread, and thus becomes yet another Peakland plant at the very limit of its viability.

Among the southern-type animals at the northern edge of their range are the nuthatch, that dashing acrobat of the tree trunk, and coming from the opposite direction, the reintroduced mountain or blue hare, at its southernmost limit on the Dark Peak moors. Our changing climate has had an unfortunate effect on the mountain hare's innate ability to change the colour of its coat to white in an attempt at better camouflage during the winter months. Ironically, the rarity of lasting winter snows these days means that the hares are rendered more, rather than less, conspicious by their change in colouration when seen against the choco-late-brown peat. Nevertheless, these handsome, rabbit-sized, darting animals which were reintroduced after extinction by shooting during the nineteenth cen-tury, seem to have enjoyed something of a comeback, and are now a common sight, especially on the moors above the Eastern Edges.

Amazingly, probably the most famous and beautiful dale of all – Dovedale, first proposed as a separate National Park in the 1930s and later as an NNR in 1947 – remains unprotected by an official designation. Having said that, it is probably safe from unsuitable development under the enlightened, conservation-first ownership of the National Trust.

Today more than half of the 555 square miles of the National Park is further protected by special environmental designations, such as Environmentally Sensitive Areas (ESAs) and Sites of Special Scientific Interest (SSSIs). The Park

*Overleaf: A high summer view
across the heather-covered
expanse of Eyam Moor, looking
north towards the Hope Valley
and the Derwent Moors*

The pure White Peak rivers, such as the Bradford below Youlgreave pictured here, are usually threaded by a good bankside path, and are enormously popular with anglers. The weirs were constructed to provide spawning areas for trout

Authority prepares special ESA Conservation Plans, Wildlife Enhancement Schemes and Heritage Management Plans so that currently, 80 per cent of moorland, 22 per cent of farmland and 16 per cent of woodland in the National Park is covered by some kind of conservation agreement.

WHITE PEAK WONDERLAND

The wildlife showplaces of the Peak District are undoubtedly the glorious limestone dales of the White Peak.

A walk through a typical limestone dale in early summer – just as the leaves of the ashwoods are slowly turning green, birdsong reaches its cacophonous zenith, and the springy herb-rich turf beneath your feet is sprinkled with an amazing array of beautiful wild flowers – is one of the real joys of the Peak District for the observant naturalist.

As you descend into the dale, in the cool canopy of the ash and sycamore trees shelter some of the classic indicator species of old, semi-natural woodland, such as dog's mercury, Solomon's seal, lily of the valley and primrose. The variety of woody shrubs which thrive in these rich woodlands, the best examples of which are found in Dovedale and Lathkill Dale, are unmatched elsewhere in the Peak. They include the nationally rare mezereon, whose lovely purple-pink flowers emerge before the leaves in spring, guelder rose, bird cherry and rock whitebeam.

When you reach the riverside path which, in almost every instance is the only means of access to these narrow White Peak dales, you may be surprised to find that the river itself is missing. This is because several of the White Peak rivers which run for all or most of their lengths on the highly porous limestone, have the disturbing habit, especially in high summer, of disappearing underground through the many fissures in the rock. Examples of these are the Lathkill – the only river in the Peak which runs for the whole of its length over limestone – the Hamps and the Manifold, which regularly disappears through sinks near Beeston Tor and reappears in the resurgence in the grounds of Ilam Hall several miles downstream. When they are flowing, these limestone rivers are among the purest in the country, and they support a wide range of rare aquatic wildlife such as the 'crawkie', the local name for the freshwater crayfish – a kind of miniature lobster – which has unfortunately suffered in recent years from disease and is rarely seen today. Making a heartening comeback to some of the quieter stretches of White Peak streams and rivers however, is the equally elusive otter.

Charles Cotton, the 'Piscator' of that seventeenth century fishermens' classic *The Compleat Angler*, wrote that the Lathkill (which he knew as the Lathkin) was 'by many degrees, the purest and most transparent stream that I ever saw, either at home or abroad. And it bred, he claimed, 'the reddest and the best Trouts in England'. He named the fair Dove, his 'beloved nymph', and further eulogised:

> *Princess of rivers, how I love*
> *Upon thy flowery banks to lie,*
> *And view thy silver stream,*
> *When gilded by a summer beam*

Today, angling licences are still at a premium for these pure and productive White Peak rivers like the Dove and Lathkill.

If you are really lucky, you will at first sense rather than see the iridescent flash of the master fisherman of these fast-flowing streams, as a kingfisher darts upstream on its constant search for food. Much more likely will be the sight of the white-bibbed dipper, curtseying up and down on a favourite, white-stained rock in midstream, for all the world like a fussy waiter poised to take your order. Then it

will suddenly disappear underwater in its search for water beetles or insect larvae, which are found as it walks, head down and facing into the current, on the riverbed. Another common sight bobbing up and down by these limestone rivers is the grey wagtail, whose mundane name does no justice to its brilliantly-coloured sulphur-yellow breast.

The bright, blue-bellied dragonflies and hoverflies which flit across the clear surface of the river are examples of the rich invertebrate life of the river which, of course, is the main attraction for these riverside birds.

Eventually, as you continue your typical dale walk upstream, you will emerge into

JACOB'S LADDER

The rugged, crag-bound upper reaches of Lathkill Dale, east of Monyash, is the home of one of the Peak District's real floral rarities. In the damp, cool dale bottom, just upstream from Lathkill Head Cave where the river emerges spectacularly in winter, one of the largest natural stands of Jacob's ladder anywhere in the country gladdens the eye in late summer. The plant, with its beautiful deep blue flowers with their golden-yellow stamens, take its name from the pinnated, fern-like leaves, which are said to represent Jacob's Biblical ladder which transported him to heaven.

Above: Jacob's ladder

Far left: The dipper (pictured) and grey wagtail are both common sights on White Peak rivers, both feeding on aquatic insects (Mark Hamblin); (left) the common blue butterfly feeds on bird's foot trefoil and other lime-loving plants in White Peak dales

the sunlit open, upper reaches, where the short, sheep-cropped turf present one of the richest floral tapestries to be found anywhere in Britain. Over 50 species have been identified in a square metre of this herb-rich grassland, including flowers like the nationally rare Nottingham catchfly, rockrose, bloody cranesbill, dark red helleborine and herb Paris. In early summer, the steeper slopes of the dales are stained red with the mysterious tall spikes of early purple orchids, while the yellow and purple 'faces' of mountain pansy and the soft pink of thyme brighten the sward beneath.

In their turn, these flower-rich grasslands support a wide range of invertebrates, including the northern brown argus, green-veined white and orange tip butterflies. Recent years have seen regular invasions of clouded yellow and painted lady butterflies from the Continent, and Lathkill Dale is the venue of a regular summertime butterfly transect monitoring exercise, which feeds into a national survey by English Nature.

Here and there, on the White Peak plateau, the naturalist can still find areas of interest in what is a largely 'improved' and enclosed landscape of monotonously green, short-term, rye-grass leys which are regularly ploughed and then re-seeded. But you can still occasionally find old-fashioned hay meadows, bright with wildflowers, where grants from the National Park Authority encourage farmers to continue to manage them in the traditional way. However, the sad fact is that as much as 75 per cent of them have either been lost entirely or have seriously deteriorated in the last ten years, and the Park's Farm and Countryside Service is struggling manfully with limited funds to try to reverse this trend. Although the future of some 150 flower-rich meadows has been secured, at least 250 still remain unprotected and at the mercy of the hard economics of food production.

A floral speciality of the White Peak plateau are the specialist range of plants which colonise the man-made habitats formed from the centuries of lead mining which have scarred these wide pastures. Most plants and flowers cannot tolerate the high concentrations of lead in the spoil heaps which still mark the old lead mining sites – but there are several notable exceptions.

One is the spring sandwort – known locally as leadwort for obvious reasons – which forms dense circular clumps at places like Magpie Mine, near Sheldon, covering the old spoil heaps in snow-like drifts. It was first recorded by the pioneering botanist John Ray in 1688, as 'in Derbyshire, on the barren earth they dig out of the shafts of lead mines' so it has been around for some time.

Confusingly also known locally as leadwort is alpine penny cress, a taller, fleshier-leaved plant, but other more common species, such as bird's foot trefoil, eyebright, sorrel and the mountain pansy have also shown they can be remarkably tolerant of these potentially toxic habitats.

Birdlife on the White Peak plateau is not as rich as in the dales, but waders such as lapwing and curlew though on the decrease because of farming improvements, are not uncommon. Skylarks still trill their silver corkscrews of song up into the summer skies, and the migrant wheatears will flash their eponymous white rumps (the name comes from the Old English 'white-arse') and scold any passing walker who inadvertently strays into their stone-walled territories.

The railway trails, such as the Tissington, High Peak and Monsal Trails, have created their own interesting, sheltered mini-habitats on the limestone plateau, where bloody cranesbill, kidney vetch and Nottingham catchfly thrive on the embankments where steam trains once passed. These embankments form useful homes for burying animals such as the badger, fox and rabbit, while weasels make their homes in the many drystone walls which criss-cross the plateau.

Top: Spring sandwort is known locally as leadwort
Centre: The haunting call of the curlew and tumbling flight of the lapwing (pictured) were both once characteristic of the White Peak plateau, but both birds have suffered declines because of changes in agricultural practices (Mark Hamblin)
Above: Wheatears flash their white rumps angrily at passing walkers (Mark Hamblin)

Opposite: The sides of the dales, such as here in upper Cressbrook Dale, near Peter's Stone (right), are covered in early purple orchids in early summer

Top: The fluffy white heads of cotton grass add movement and variety to the otherwise bleak and forbidding Dark Peak landscape of peat hags and groughs

Above: The delicate purple-pink flowers of the bilberry precede the delicious berries, and favour drier parts of the moorland

LAND AT THE END OF ITS TETHER

The late John Hillaby, walker and naturalist, memorably described the Dark Peak moors of Kinder Scout, Bleaklow and Black Hill in his *Journey through Britain*:

'From the botanical point of view, they are examples of land at the end of its tether. All the life has been drained off or burnt out, leaving behind only the acid peat. You can find nothing like them anywhere else in Europe.'

The moors of the Dark Peak represent the nearest thing to a wilderness in the National Park, although even these have been created by centuries of Man's grazing and burning. The rolling moonscape of chocolate brown hags (banks) and groughs (natural drainage channels) of peat which stretch for mile after mile north of Edale, gently steaming after a summer shower of rain, reminded Hillaby of nothing more than 'the droppings of dinosaurs'. The only sound he heard was the mournful cheeping of the ubiquitous meadow pipits, sounding 'like the last ticks of a clock that has almost run down'.

Unpromising though they may seem, the Dark Peak moors are important in natural history terms as one of the few remaining examples of blanket bog in Europe. And in their detail, there are many surprising examples of wildlife which thrive in the apparently hostile environment of the high, peat moors.

The fluffy white fruiting heads of cotton grass, which enliven so many moorland views in summer, have given their name to the many 'Featherbed Mosses' of the Pennines, including the one south of the Snake Road between Kinder Scout and Bleaklow. In the boggiest, less well-drained areas, the bright apple green of sphagnum moss – the major agent in the creation of the peat over many centuries – is a tell-tale sign for the rambler to watch his or her step. And here and there, you might come across the brilliant yellow flowers of bog asphodel, one of the gems of the high moors.

On the drier, better-drained, sections of the moors, woody plants such as heather, bilberry and crowberry can be found in springy carpets. The sight of a well-managed heather moor, glorious in its royal purple hue in late summer, is one of the finest experiences for the Dark Peak walker. But even this is the careful creation of landowners who created it to provide bed and board for a single, very important, bird.

The single most important reason for the wonderful heather moors of the Dark Peak is the red grouse, the nearest thing we have to an exclusively British bird, and the objective of every self-respecting shooter after the Glorious Twelfth of August every year. Red grouse, whose croaking 'Go back, go back, back, back' call is such a distinctive part of any moorland ramble, need young heather shoots to feed on, and older, more woody plants in which to roost and nest. The systematic burning of old heather in the spring creates that distinctive, patchwork-quilt mosaic of heather which they require.

It's been a long time since during the heyday of grouse shooting, a record 1,421½ brace (2,843 birds) were shot on Broomhead Moor in 1913, and there's not so much shooting of grouse these days, as the population has suffered badly from disease. But make no mistake, the heather moors would not be the treasure that they are if it were not for that furry-footed, plump game bird. A rarer member of the grouse family, decimated by habitat destruction, the black grouse or blackcock is now limited to a few pairs which cling on in a single site in the Staffordshire Moorlands.

The waders of the high moors include the spangle-feathered golden plover, often known as 'the watchman of the moors', the curved-beak curlew and, more rarely the dotterel. The steep-sided rocky 'cloughs' which drain the high moors are haunted by the 'chinking' call of the ring ouzel or mountain blackbird, together with grey wagtails and dippers.

In direct contrast with the waders and the black grouse, the birds of prey which quarter the high moors have shown encouraging signs of revival since their numbers crashed in the pesticide-poisoning scares of the 1950s. Top of the list of Dark

Above: The white breast of the ring ouzel or mountain blackbird is often seen in moorland cloughs, where this summer visitor makes its nest

Left: The handsome golden plover is known as 'the watchman of the moors' from the distinctive, musical warning call it sounds on the approach of intruders (Both photographs Mark Hamblin)

Peak raptors is the dashing peregrine falcon, which returned to breed in a couple of top secret locations after an absence of thirty years during the 1990s. Birdwatchers were also heartened to see the return of hen harriers to the Goyt Valley in 1997, but populations of the small, thrush-sized merlin and the bold, buccaneering goshawk, which has its British stronghold in the conifers which surround the reservoirs of the Upper Derwent Valley, appear to be static.

The deep valleys of the Dark Peak, so close to the teeming cities either side, have long attracted the water engineers seeking clean drinking water, and there are over fifty reservoirs in the area. Again, on the surface they may look unpromsing as habitats for wildlife, but in fact they support a surprising amount, from the red-breasted mergansers, among the few birds which seem to enjoy the deep, acid waters, to the dashing goshawks which haunt the surrounding belts of conifer forestry. Here too can be seen tiny goldcrests, siskins in winter, and the occasional summer 'eruption' of crossbills.

But the conifer plantations cannot compare with wildlife interest of the native woodlands of the Dark Peak, such as the sessile oakwoods of the Derbyshire Wildlife Trust's reserve at Ladybower Wood and the National Trust's Padley Gorge, near Grindleford. Padley is particularly noted for its summer population of pied flycatchers, resplendent in their stunning black and white plumage, while other resident birds include greater spotted and green woodpeckers, redstarts, treecreepers and nuthatches, on the very edge of their range here, as stated above. The mammals of the Dark Peak include the re-introduced mountain hare and the common fox and badger, but the most magnificent – and largest – are the majestic red deer which lord it over the rough parklands of Lyme Hall, near Stockport, and Chatsworth, in the valley of the Derwent, which also has a resident herd of fallow deer.

Above: The peregrine falcon has enjoyed something of a comeback on Dark Peak moors

Opposite: Britain's largest land mammal, a red deer stag roars its challenge to rivals during the autumnal rut
Below: Watch out for this character when out walking the moor: the adder – a stunner in every sense!
(All photographs Mark Hamblin)

3 Man's influence

Opposite: Looking out onto Wetton Hill from the interior of Thor's Cave above the Manifold Valley in Staffordshire. This view has not changed much since Stone Age man used it as a shelter 5,000 years ago

Note the climbers' sling hanging from the lip of the roof. This impressive route is known as Thormen's Moth

The short, stocky man clad in deerskins looked out from under deep-browed eyes from the dark recesses of the cave entrance high above the deeply-incised valley. Just below him, a herd of majestic reindeer grazed peacefully on the cold, dry grassland which spread down towards the marshy valley floor. Soon he would be setting out with other members of the band to try to ambush them. A reindeer carcass would provide the family band with the valuable meat, clothing and material to make the bone tools which they needed to survive in their harsh, cold environment. He prayed to his Gods that they would be successful.

This scene could have been repeated in any of several sites in the Peak District, including Thor's Fissure Cave, Elder Bush Cave and Ossum's Cave in the Manifold Valley, where evidence of the first Palaeolithic hunter-gatherers has been found by archaeologists. Nearby, at Creswell Crags on the borders of Nottinghamshire, further evidence of Palaeolithic man has been found, including the first examples of art in Britain, a horse's head engraved on an antler.

When these first Peaklanders crossed the land bridge from Europe in the wake of the retreating glaciers at the end of the last Ice Age, they looked out on a primeval landscape very different from that of today. They would have followed the herds of reindeer as they headed north in summer in search of fresh pasturage on the sub-Arctic tundra which was slowly emerging from the grip of the icesheets. And they would have collected roots, tubers, leaves, nuts and berries to eat through to autumn in the sparse scrubland which was gradually establishing itself into the virgin forest of the wildwood.

Evidence of these first settlers in what we now know as the Peak District is sparse and hard to find, but by 5,000 years ago, Mesolithic, or Middle Stone Age, people were already making substantial alterations to the gradually warming landscape they had inherited. Hunting parties now spread out onto the higher ground, which by now was thickly forested in oak, birch and lime. One of my most prized possessions is a tiny sliver of flint, no bigger than my little fingernail, which I picked up from the side of a peat hag on Black Hill many years ago. Known to archaeologists as a microlith, it once formed part of a primitive arrowhead used by a Mesolithic hunter. It still gives me a thrill to realise that I was the first person to pick it up from where it had fallen 5,000 years ago, perhaps after an unsuccessful shot at a fleeing deer when Black Hill was still covered in the wildwood forest.

The first farmers emerged on the Peak District scene during the Neolithic – or New Stone Age – period, between 4,500 and 2000BC. Again, it is only through the scattered remains of their stone tools, and the few rare reminders of their mysterious ritual monuments and where they buried their dead, that we can reconstruct their lives. The only Neolithic settlement site which has been so far discovered in the Peak District as in the valley of the Wye at Lismore Fields, west of Buxton.

The most famous Neolithic site in the Peak District is undoubtedly Arbor Low, sometimes dubbed 'the Stonehenge of the North', and dating from exactly the same period as its much better-known Wiltshire contemporary. It stands just off the minor road between Youlgreave and the A515 at Parsley Hay on a broad plateau at 1,230ft (375m) above the sea, commanding extensive views across the

Top: This aerial view shows the 'clockface' layout of the fallen stones at Arbor Low inside the 5,000-year-old 160ft (48m) diameter henge monument

Above: Cows peacefully graze around the fallen stones and embankments of Arbor Low, perhaps the most important prehistoric site in the Peak District, near Parsley Hay

White Peak plateau towards the northern moors. Arbor Low consists of a large henge 160ft (48m) in diameter and about 7ft (2m) in height, on the south-eastern corner of which has been superimposed a Bronze Age barrow.

In the centre of the henge lies a circle of about fifty large prostrate limestone slabs, apparently spread out on the flower-decked greensward like the figures on a clock-face. For many years, archaeologists argued as to whether these massive stones ever stood upright – as with every other stone circle in Britain. But by the 1990s, opinion was at last reconciled that they must have, when it was discovered that some of the stones were in fact the broken-off stumps of their neighbours which had been cast down at some time in their 5,000-year history.

At the centre of the circle are two or three massive stones known to archaeologists as a 'cove'. The Victorian antiquary H. St George Gray, in 1901 discovered a human burial under one of these stones, which are thought to have been the sacred, central focus of the monument – although what it was used for, no one really knows.

There is another, even earlier Neolithic monument at Arbor Low, and that is the neighbouring long barrow of Gib Hill, a couple of fields away to the south. This was probably built around 3,000BC and also later had a large Bronze Age barrow superimposed upon it, proving the lasting importance these monuments to generations of prehistoric people.

You can still feel something of the magic of Arbor Low as you stand on its ancient henge on a still, summer's evening, when the only sound is the spiralling song of the skylark and the gentle munching of grazing cows around your feet. It is an experience sadly lost to visitors to Stonehenge, with its ugly car park, visitor centre and tunnel. At Arbor Low, you are still allowed to experience and interpret the monument for yourself.

All around you is the tangible evidence of that prehistoric past, for on almost every hilltop as you look round the vast spreading panorama, you can make out the tiny pimple which indicates yet another burial mound, or 'low', most of which date from the Bronze Age. And beneath you, the enigmatic stone circle still refuses to give up its age-old secrets.

Arbor Low is one of two Neolithic henge monuments known in the Peak District. The other, now robbed of its stones if it ever had them, is the Bull Ring above Dove Holes, north of Buxton. The best guess is that these mysterious monuments were the major communial sites of their day, probably used for seasonal ceremonial events by people from all over the district.

Until recently, historians believed that the only Stone Age settlement of the Peak District was on the high and dry limestone plateau. But recent excavations on Gardom's Edge, on the moors above Baslow, have revealed an extensive defended

The enigmatic cup-and-ring carved boulder discovered below Gardom's Edge, near Baslow, has been replaced by this modern replica to protect the original. No one is sure what the markings signified to the Bronze Age people who carved them, but the boulder lay at the centre of an extensive settlement which had been occupied since Neolithic times

A WAY OF DEATH

We know much more about the way Neolithic people buried their leaders than how they lived. There are eight examples of Neolithic chambered cairns, which were mounds containing burial chambers built of large stone slabs and simple stone-sided boxes or 'cists'. The best-known of these, and one of the biggest in the country, is the Five Wells chambered cairn overlooking the valley of the Wye. Its siting, at over 1,410ft (430m) is significant, as it was obviously designed to overlook and overawe the local population. At least twelve burials were made in it, and it is thought that the bones were taken out for ceremonial purposes at certain times of the year. Another Neolithic chambered cairn in a highly-prominent position is Minninglow, standing at 1,220ft (372m) above the High Peak Trail between Parwich and Elton. Its straggly cupola of ancient beech trees is a constant landmark in so many views across the White Peak plateau, as the mound of the chambered cairn must have been for centuries before they were planted.

Winter view of the Five Wells Neolithic chambered tomb above the A6 near Taddington, the highest such monument in the country

Hidden behind a curtain of winter birches, the Nine Ladies stone circle on Stanton Moor is another ritual or religious site dating from the Bronze Age. Over seventy burial mounds as well as other stone circles have been identified in the surrounding moorland, making it one of the most important prehistoric sites in the district

enclosure dating from the Neolithic period and the largest of its kind in northern England. It is surrounded by later field systems, house sites, stone circles and clearance cairns which date from the Bronze Age, and which are superimposed over the enclosure, proving its earlier date.

There was certainly a move from the limestone to the gritstone of the Dark Peak during the Bronze Age, and entire landscapes dating from the Bronze Age (between 3,000 and 4000 years ago) have been revealed, fossilised under the moor-grass, in many places on the Eastern Edges of the Peak District. These include the important sites of Swine Sty and Barbrook, on the National Park Authority's Eastern Moors estate.

As stated earlier, one of the many paradoxes of the Peak District is that where you see the name 'low' it is normally on a high point. Over 500 of these 'lows' have been identified in the district and in nearly every case, they mark a burial mound usually dating from the Late Neolithic or Early Bronze Age. Many of these barrows were excavated by the pioneering archaeologist Thomas Bateman of Middleton-by-Youlgreave in the 1840s and 1850s. Thankfully, Bateman recorded most of what he found and many of his finds are now safely housed in the Weston Park Museum in nearby Sheffield.

Bateman and his colleague Samuel Carrington also excavated many of the stone circles dating from the Bronze Age, such as Nine Stones on Harthill Moor and the

Nine Ladies circle on Stanton Moor. Stanton Moor, a gritstone outlier overlooking the Derwent Valley south of Bakewell, has been described as a Bronze Age 'necropolis' because more than seventy burial mounds have been identified beneath its heather, in addition to the Nine Ladies and other stone circles.

Eventually, the Bronze Age which lasted between 2,100 to 650BC slipped imperceptibly into the Iron Age. It is thought the climate became steadily colder and wetter, and many of the more exposed farmsteads, such as those on the Eastern Moors, were abandoned in favour of the more sheltered conditions in the valleys. But the hill pastures were still important for summer grazing, and the eight Iron Age 'hillforts' which have been identified in the Peak District are thought to have been used for at least some of the time as summer sheilings to watch over these flocks. The term 'hillfort' was a Victorian invention, and archaeologists now consider that it puts an overly-military emphasis on their interpretation. Certainly, the solid defences of places like Mam Tor, overlooking the head of the Hope Valley, may well have had a military function, but there is no archaeological evidence of conflict.

The common theory that these forts were built by retreating Ancient Britons as a last stronghold against the advancing Roman legions is far from the truth. The lack of Later Iron Age earthworks in the Peak District hillforts seems to indicate that they had been abandoned long before the Romans arrived.

Low sun highlights the cultivation terraces of the Romano-British settlement at Chee Tor above the valley of the River Wye

TOWNS IN THE AIR

Mam Tor, standing at 1,695ft (517m) is one of the largest and most imposing hillforts in Britain, covering 16 acres (6ha) and dotted with a large number of circular hut sites. It is now thought that the massive ramparts of the fort were built up to the famous 'shivering' east face of the mountain, and not swept away by the famous landslip. Other notable Iron Age hillforts in the Peak include Burr Tor, on the site of the gliding club above Great Hucklow; Castle Naze, above Chapel-en-le-Frith, and the only one yet discovered on the limestone, Fin Cop, which overlooks the Wye at Monsal Head, near Ashford-in-the-Water. The massive walls and easily defensible site of Carl Wark, above Hathersage, has still not conclusively been dated to the Iron Age, and may be much earlier

Right: Looking down on the mysterious fortification of Carl Wark from Higger Tor in the valley of the Burbage Brook above Hathersage, whose date and purpose still eludes archaeologists

BAKEWELL'S SUMMIT

Bakewell was the scene in 920AD, of an historic meeting called in a specially-constructed 'burh' or fortification, by King Edward the Elder, Alfred's oldest son. Here, the kings of the Scots, Northumbria and Strathclyde, accepted him as their 'father and lord', in what was in effect the first unification of the nation of England. This was also the period in which the district received its name, for it was populated by a tribe called the Pecsaete – the people of the Peak. The Old English meaning of the word peac was a knoll or hill, and not the modern one of a sharply-pointed summit.

The largest of Bakewell's vigorously carved preaching crosses, now in the churchyard; these were probably made by a local school of sculptors

It was the copious and easily-obtained supplies of lead which probably attracted the Romans into the inhospitable hills of the Peak District in the late 70s AD. The forts of *Navio*, on a bend overlooking the River Noe near Brough in the Hope Valley, and *Ardotalia*, now known as Melandra, near Glossop, are the main evidence for this. The site of the lead mining centre of *Lutodarum*, whose name has been identified on several Roman pigs of lead, has still to be discovered. There was also the important urban site of *Aquae Arnemetiae* at Buxton, founded on the warm springs which issue from the limestone here.

Recent investigations have uncovered a previously-unsuspected wealth of evidence of Romano-British farmsteads in the White Peak area. This is particularly true at Roystone Grange, near Ballidon, where students from Sheffield University have conducted a ten-year programme which revealed evidence of farming activities from the second to fourth centuries through to the present day. Some of the 'orthostat' drystone walls still in use at Roystone have even been dated to that Romano-British period.

After the Roman legions finally left, the Peak District and the rest of Britain was plunged into what former historians have somewhat unfairly been dubbed 'the Dark Ages'. In fact, this period of Anglian and Saxon rule saw a flowering of art and culture which, in the Peak District, is chiefly marked by the finest collection of Saxon preaching crosses outside Northumbria. The best examples are at Bakewell, where there are two eighth century crosses in the churchyard and a collection of other Saxon and medieval carved stones in the porch. Bakewell was known to have a monastery in the mid-tenth century, which could well have housed a school of sculptors which produced the other finely-carved crosses in the district such as those at Eyam, Ilam, Hope and Bradbourne. The seventh century burial uncovered by Bateman at Benty Grange, near Parsley Hay, marks one of the earliest signs of the coming of Christianity to the Peak, for the warrior was buried with his fine helmet which included both Christian and pagan motifs in its decoration.

Bakewell's preeminence was further confirmed in the Domesday Survey, written just twenty years after William the Conqueror's invasion. It is recorded as having thirty-three villagers and nine smallholders, a man-at-arms and a church with the rare privilege of two priests, as well as a mill and a lead mine.

But the greatest Norman and medieval monument in the Peak is without doubt the castle which gave Castleton its name, built by William Peveril. The earliest parts of Peveril Castle date from the twelfth century, and the commanding keep, on the impregnable rocky peninsula between the Peak Cavern gorge and Cave Dale, was built for £200 in 1175-76. Its main purpose was to govern the Royal Forest of the Peak – a 40sq mile (103sq km) wilderness between the Etherow and the Wye set aside for the hunting pleasures of successive medieval kings. The planned medieval market town of Castleton also dates from this period, but it never filled the boundaries laid down by its still-surviving Town Ditch.

Much of the north of the area had been recorded in Domesday as *wasta est* or 'it was waste', which may have been the result of the Conqueror's savage 'Harrying of the North', or more likely, the result of the general economic depression which followed the uncertainty of the Conquest.

Further south, market towns like Tideswell prospered on the wealth being won from lead and wool, and 'Tidser' was granted the right to hold a weekly market as early as 1251. Tideswell's magnificent parish church of St John the Baptist – often known as 'the Cathedral of the Peak' – is one of the finest in the country, built during the transition period between the Decorated to the Perpendicular style in fifty

years between 1320 and 1370. Other towns and villages were not so successful, and there are deserted medieval village sites at Nether Haddon, Conksbury and Smerrel.

The great landowning families of the Peak – the Eyres, Leghs, Manners, Vernons and Cavendishes – also gained much of their enormous wealth from the dual economies of farming and mineral extraction. With it, they built their fine mansions of North Lees, Lyme Park, Haddon Hall and Chatsworth, which now attract visitors from all over the world. The fine landscaped parklands of Lyme, Haddon and Chatsworth have made significant contributions to the landscape of the Peak, while the fine eighteenth century buildings of Buxton, such as The Crescent, the Natural Baths and the Royal Devonshire Hospital are all said to have been built on the huge profits made by the Duke of Devonshire from his lead and copper-mining interests in the Peak.

Lead mining in the Peak, started by the Romans, probably reached its hey-day between 1700 and 1750, when at least 10,000 miners were at work burrowing beneath the limestone. The lead mining industry contributed a great deal to the economy and culture of the region, and some of its colourful language is still in common use, such as the 'nicking' of a mine and the description of old mine workings and miners as 't'owd man'.

The best preserved and most impressive remains of a lead mine are at Magpie

The Elizabethan towerhouse of North Lees Hall, on the moors above Hathersage, was one of seven built by Robert Eyre for his sons, and was later used by Charlotte Brontë as the model for Thornfield Hall in Jane Eyre

The history of man's settlement in the Hope Valley in one picture. In the background the sheer east face of Mam Tor stands below the embankments of the late Bronze Age/early Iron Age hillfort, which can just be made out on the skyline. William Peveril's four-square Norman keep fills the foreground, perched on the virtually impregnable crags of Cave Dale

Above: The Monsal Dale viaduct from Monsal Head – subject of John Ruskin's wrath when the Midland line was constructed through the valley of the River Wye in 1860

Opposite: The magnificent Georgian country house structure of Cressbrook Mill in Cressbrook Dale was built in 1815, replacing an earlier cotton mill built by Richard Arkwright which burned down

Mine, near Sheldon, now a scheduled ancient monument and field study centre for the thriving Peak District Mines Historical Society. Magpie was worked more or less continuously for 200 years, and its remaining buildings show various stages of the development of the industry, from the square Derbyshire chimney to the round Cornish one, and the chapel-like ruins of the nineteenth-century engine house.

It was copper, not lead, which was the major objective for the Duke of Devonshire's mines at Ecton Hill, in the Manifold Valley of Staffordshire. In one year, 1786, about 4,000 tons of copper ore was extracted from the incredibly-rich pipe veins, and the Duke was said to have made a total profit of £1.3 million from the mines.

One of the greatest problems facing the lead and copper miners in the Peak was water, and thousands of pounds were spent on 'de-watering' the mines by constructing long 'soughs' to drain them. But that fast-flowing water was the attraction to the first mill-builders, such as Richard Arkwright and Jedediah Strutt, who were the first to harness the power of rivers like the Derwent and Wye to power the first cotton factories of the Industrial Revolution. The earliest Arkwright mills were at Cromford, Cressbrook and Bakewell, and the present Cressbrook Mill, a handsome, pedimented Georgian building dating from 1815, is one of the finest examples of its kind in the country.

As communications improved across the Peak's 'howling wilderness', the old packhorse routes used by the 'jaggers' or leaders of the trains of horses, were gradually replaced by turnpike roads such as Thomas Telford's route across the Snake Pass, opened in 1821.

The Railway Age came surprisingly early to the hills of the Peak District with the construction of the Cromford and High Peak Railway across the 1,000ft (300m) White Peak limestone plateau in 1830. Originally envisaged, amazingly, as a canal, it was designed to link the Cromford Canal with the Peak Forest Canal at Whaley Bridge, and was originally horse-powered with stationery steam engines to haul to waggons up the steep inclines at either end of the 33-mile route.

The Midland line linking London and Manchester followed in 1860, and was one of the most ambitious railway projects of its day. A whole series of viaducts, tunnels and cuttings swept it through the Wye Valley, exciting the wrath of John Ruskin, who roundly condemned the means by which 'every fool in Buxton can be at Bakewell in half an hour and every fool in Bakewell at Buxton'. The route is now the Monsal Trail, and there are long-term plans to re-open it to passenger and freight traffic, retaining the popular footpath route. The Cromford and High Peak line is now the High Peak Trail, running parallel to the Tissington Trail, once the short-lived Buxton-Ashbourne line.

4 Land use, culture and customs

When Celia Fiennes, the intrepid daughter of a Roundhead colonel, undertook her lone journey *Through England on a Side Saddle in the time of William and Mary* in the late seventeenth and early eighteenth centuries, the Derbyshire Peak District was a wild, largely unknown place. Her description of the landscape, however, is still instantly recognisable today:

'All Derbyshire is full of steep hills, and nothing but the peakes of hills as thick one by another is seen in most of the County which are very steepe which makes travelling tedious, and the miles long, you see neither hedge nor tree but only low drye stone walls round some ground, else its only hills and dales as thick as you can imagine.'

Later, as she entered 'Bankwell' (Bakewell) from Chatsworth, she noted: '…it stands on a hill yet you descend a vast hill to it, which you would thinke impossible to go down and we was forced to fetch a great compass, and by reason of the steepness and hazard of the Wayes – if you take a wrong Way there is no passing – you are forced to have Guides as in all parts of Darbyshire.'

Those 'low drye stone walls' are still the abiding first impression of the

Below: '…you see neither hedge nor tree but only drye stone walls…' Celia Fiennes' seventeenth-century view still holds good today as in this typical scene of Enclosure Movement walls on the White Peak plateau near Litton

Peak District, especially to travellers approaching from the south of England. Spreading across the swelling contours like a stony net, up hill and down dale, they represent many years of patient, back-breaking labour, and tell us much of the history of farming in the Peak.

Most of these walls are the result of the Parliamentary Enclosure Movement of the eighteenth and nineteenth centuries which totally transformed the English landscape, causing exactly the same sort of out-cry then which today greets the grubbing out of what are often the same walls and hedgerows. In an early example of privatisation, Parliamentary surveyors par-celled up the common land and awarded it to those who could afford to enclose it, who were obviously usually the larger landowners.

The Northamptonshire nature poet, John Clare, roundly condemned the loss of what was once common land, available to all:

Inclosure, thou'rt curse upon the land
And tasteless was the wretch who thy existence planned.

Another popular rhyme of the time exposed the bitter irony and sorely-felt injustice of the situation:

They hang the man and flog the woman
Who steals the goose from off the common.
But let the greater criminal loose
Who steals the common from the goose.

Before the Enclosures, which neatly partitioned the country up into a tight gridwork of walls and hedgerows, the Peak District, as other parts of the country, operated the open field system of agriculture, which dated from at least the early medieval period and pos-sibly much earlier. Under this age-old system, villagers split their land into an 'infield' and an 'outfield'.

The infield lay close to the village and consisted of strips of land, known as tofts, running back from the crofts or houses of the villagers. These long, narrow strips are nowadays often 'fossilised' by being enclosed by later drystone walls, as in the classic case of Chelmorton, 1,000ft/300m up on the limestone plateau 4 miles south east of Buxton. The Chelmorton walls are so typical and famous that many are now protected by special management agreements with the National Park Authority, but there are many other good examples, such as at Taddington, Monyash and around Tideswell. In many cases, the slight 'reversed S' shape of these narrow strip fields still reveals the wide swing which was needed to turn the eight-strong teams of oxen which originally ploughed the land. That 'reversed S' can also been seen in the corrugated ridge-and-furrowed fields in the south of the district, especially well seen from the A515 near Tissington, particularly in the low light of evening or after a fresh fall of snow.

Top: Aided by grants from the National Park Authority, drystone walling is no longer a dying art. This drystone waller plies his ancient craft as he encloses a new plantation
Above: Haymaking creates linear patterns in these limestone pastures near Bretton. Although much grass is now cut for silage, haymaking is still important to many Peak District farmers stocking up feed for their livestock during the long, hard winter

Overleaf: The distinctive sweeping 'reversed S' of medieval ridge-and-furrow cultivation is well seen in this view of the fields near Elton

Beyond the cultivated infield of the village lay the more extensive outfield, where the villagers' stock grazed during the summer months on the common land which earlier farmers had won from the moorland. It was the loss of this traditionally commonly-held land which so enraged John Clare and others.

Recent investigations by Sheffield University in partnership with the National Park authority at Roystone Grange, just north of Ballidon, have shown that the 'infield-outfield' system may be very early. Archaeologists have identified a clearly defined infield and outfield enclosed by 2,000-year-old Romano-British 'orthostat' walls, many of which are still in use. The enclosed area nearest to the settlement was used for cultivation and the outfield for the grazing of stock, just as in the medieval period.

Top: Grazing beef cattle are a common sight on Peak District pastures, which are often now converted to short-term leys of ryegrass

Roystone is one of about fifty granges which have been identified in the Peak District, which were outlying stock farms, usually great sheep ranches of monasteries in the Midlands and the north of England, which produced the economically valuable 'golden fleece' of the Middle Ages. These monkish entrepreneurs were the first of a series of autocratic farming landlords who were to impose their wills, and their walls, across the Peak District landscape, the last of which were the Parliamentary enclosers.

Below: The National Park Authority tries to encourage the retention of herb-rich flower meadows, like this one near Sparrowpit, through its Farm and Countryside Service

Farming is still the major industry of the Peak District and the one which has largely shaped the landscape which so many visitors love today. It is also arguably the idustry which has done the least amount of harm to that cherished landscape. Pastoral farming and the raising of livestock is the chief enterprise of Peak District

farmers, as it has been for at least 5,000 years. On the limestone plateau of the White Peak, the most typical scene is of herds of black-and-white Friesian dairy cattle peacefully grazing on short-term, grassy leys. The traditional flower-starred and herb-rich hay meadows are sadly now largely a thing of the past. In the last decade, 75 per cent have either disppeared or deteriorated, although the National Park Authority's Hay Meadows Project under its Farm and Countryside Service has done its best by managing to secure the immediate future of 150 of them. Others are protected under Conservation Plans or Wildlife Enhancement Schemes under the South West Peak Environmentally Sensitive Area.

Some of the milk from those dairy herds still finds its way into traditional Stilton cheese-making at the factory at Hartington, one of a handful in the country which is entitled to make this strong, blue-veined, 'King of English Cheeses'. But at one time, most farms made their own cheese and butter for local sale, and surplus milk was transported by railways like the ill-fated Buxton-Ashbourne line and the Manifold and Leek Light Railway to the surrounding towns and cities. Today, milk tankers do the same job, extracting the milk from refrigerated bulk tanks on their daily runs through the stone-walled lanes.

Other White Peak pastures and most of the Dark Peak moors are populated by vast flocks of black-faced sheep, just as they have been since medieval times. Sheep farmers, like most others, have been having a hard time of it in recent years, and prices at the weekly markets at Bakewell and Hope have been greatly depressed. But it is still the nibbling teeth of sheep which are the major agents in shaping the landscape of most of the Peak District. Photographs of the White Peak dales taken at the turn of the century graphically illustrate the effect that grazing can have on the landscape. Then, while huge flocks of sheep still grazed the dale floors, the dramatic rock features of places like Dovedale were clearly visible whereas today, with the sheep driven from the dale by hordes of visitors, they are effectively masked by verdant tree growth. It is ironic that when bodies like the National Trust or the National Park Authority cut back these invasive trees, their actions usually attract vigorous criticism.

The traditional dual economy of the Peak District during historic times has always been farming and mining. But the last of the lead mines closed about fifty years ago and today's miners are either quarrymen or engaged in extracting the fluorspar which the old lead miners threw away as waste. There are still about fifty active quarries in the National Park, the largest of which still extract limestone from huge excavations like those at Ballidon and Tunstead. There can be no doubt that these huge holes and their associated lorry traffic do tremendous harm to the protected landscape of the National Park. One of the concerns of the National Park Authority, when it opposes extensions to these blots on the landscape, is that although Peak limestone is extremely pure calcium carbonate, the rock is not used for chemical purposes which might militate for its use, but usually ends up under tarmac as road aggregate.

However, as mechanisation proceeds and the road-building industry goes into decline, less people are employed in quarrying today than in the tourism and service industries. So as the economic base of the district has changed, so its dependence on the mineral wealth of the Peak has declined.

Some of the old former lead mining 'rakes' are still being worked for fluorspar, which is used in the chemical industry, in steel production and as a whitener, and proposals for a major underground mine at Great Hucklow were approved when the applicants resolved to dispose of their waste by back-filling in the mine.

GLORIOUS GROUSE

The other great land-shaping agent of the heather moors of the Dark Peak is a bird – the plump, furry-footed red grouse – which has been shot for sport after the 'Glorious Twelfth' of August since Victorian times. The varied, patchwork-quilt appearance of a well-managed grouse moor is quite deliberate, as areas are systematically burned during the early spring to dispose of the old, woody heather and encourage the growth of the new, young heather shoots, which are an important part of the diet of both grouse and sheep.

In fact, the glorious, purple-hued expanse of heather which is such a beautiful sight during August and September on the high moors is largely due to the gamekeepers' overiding concern for that red-wattled game bird, whose warning 'go-back, go-back, back' call usually has precisely the opposite effect on thousands of ramblers.

Above: Eldon Hill Quarry, near Castleton, earned the epithet of 'the worst eyesore in the Peak', and was actually in operation before the National Park came into being in 1951. After a long-running battle to halt further extensions, the National Park Authority won Government approval for its closure in 1995, and it is finally due to close in 2001

Left: Looking down on the Howden Dam in the Upper Derwent Valley from Abbey Bank, with the Howden Moors beyond. The Howden Reservoir was constructed between 1901 and 1912 by an army of 1,000 navvies who lived with their families in the temporary 'Tin Town' of Birchinlee, beside the Derwent Reservoir lower down the valley

Ironically, many of the old lead mining rakes now provide habitats for rare flowers and plants, and a new project by the National Park Authority seeks to protect these unusual but still fragile and threatened environments.

Several smaller quarries at places like Stanton Moor still extract gritstone for building and ornamental use, but although their size make them less of a threat to the landscape, they are locally very contentious. Government policy and legislation on mineral extraction in the National Parks remains complex, despite the provisions of the latest Environment Act. The recent Minerals Review discovered that some companies are continuing to extract minerals on planning permissions and conditions which were granted long before the National Park came into being.

Another large-scale agent of landscape change has been the fifty-odd reservoirs which have flooded many of the deep valleys of the Dark Peak. Together with the uniform belts of coniferous plantations which usually surround them, the reservoirs have been one of the most significant land use changes in the northern, eastern and western moors, creating a totally-artificial landscape which is nevertheless very popular with visitors. Starting with the string of five reservoirs in the Longdendale Valley – at the time the largest stretch of man-made water in the world – others soon followed in the rush to slake the thirsts of the burgeoning populations of the neighbouring industrial cities.

Probably the most ... the ... in the Upper Derwent – Howden,

Above: The Ladybower is the largest reservoir in the Peak District, constructed between 1935–43 to provide water for Derby, Nottingham, Leicester and Sheffield. It was the last of the series of three reservoirs built in the Upper Derwent Valley

Opposite: The cottages in Eyam where the plague first struck in 1665, with the tower of the church in the background

Derwent and Ladybower – which were built between 1901 and 1943. This area, with its 1.25 million visitors each year, is now the subject of an award-winning traffic and visitor management scheme, involving the closing of the cul-de-sac valley road at busy times, and the provision of visitor facilities, mini-buses and cycle hire. A similar scheme was pioneered at the Goyt Valley reservoirs in the west of the Park in the 1970s.

CUSTOMS AND FOLKLORE

Despite its proximity to the cities of the industrial north, the remoteness of the Peak District has tended to encourage the survival of ancient folklore and customs which have not survived elsewhere. Perhaps the best-known and most popular with visitors is the mysterious and beautiful custom of well dressing.

No one can say for sure when this unique custom started, but most authorities agree that it must originally have been a pagan Celtic ceremony to give thanks for the precious, life-giving gift of water, especially on the high and usually dry limestone plateau of the White Peak. Certainly, this is where the custom is first recorded in 1615 at Tissington, traditionally still the first the take place on Ascension Day each year.

Every summer each village in turn, often as they celebrate their local Wakes Week, prepares and decorates their local wells or springs with these intricate floral tableaux, nowadays usually with a Biblical theme. The design is pricked out in soft clay in a wooden frame and then coloured and filled in with flower petals and other natural materials gathered from the surrounding fields and gardens. The well dressings are then erected over the village spring and stand for about a week before the sun and rain starts to destroy them, and they are taken down again ready for next year.

More than thirty villages – far more than ever did in the past – now perform this annual thanksgiving, attracting huge crowds of visitors who come to admire this unique and colourful form of folk art.

A springtime custom 'lost in the mists of time' which also revolves around a floral tribute is the Castleton Garlanding, held each year on Oak Apple Day, 29 May. Dressed in Stuart period costumes, the Garland 'King' and his 'Queen' ride through the streets of the town, led by white-dressed children singing the unique Garland tune, which bears a strong resemblance to the Cornish Floral Dance and may have been introduced by Cornish tin miners. The King is crowned by a heavy wooden cone-shaped framework covered in flowers and leaves which reaches down to his waist. At the end of the tour, which visits all the village pubs in turn, the garland is hoisted to top top of the tower of the oak-decked village church, where it is left to wither and die. This may be another originally pagan fertility rite, to mark the end of winter and greet the coming of spring.

The Eyam plague commemoration service is held every August just outside the village in a rocky limestone delph known as Cucklett Church. It remembers the brave action of the villagers, led by their rector, the Rev William Mompesson and

his non-Conformist predecessor, Thomas Stanley, who imposed a quarantine on their movements when the plague struck in 1665 – so halting the spread of the dread disease to other communities. The delph was used for holding services during the time of the disease, in a further attempt to halt its spread. This heroic action saw the death of 259 villagers over two years, including Mompesson's wife, but the plague – if that is what the disease was – was contained. Today, various cottages in the village carry plaques naming those who died there during the 'visitation' of 1665–66, and a book containing the names of all who died is kept in the parish church. But perhaps the most touching memorials to the brave sacrifice made by the people of Eyam are the sad little graveyards out in the fields surrounding the village, such as the Riley Graves, where entire families were buried in unconsecrated ground.

LOLLARDS, COVENANTERS & MARTYRS

The remoteness of the Peak District attracted non-Conformists in times of religious persecution. Among these were Lollards and Covenanters who gathered in remote spots to celebrate their services. One of these was a barn at Alport Castles Farm, in the deep and isolated valley of the Alport which runs south from the boggy heights of Bleaklow, and on the first Sunday of July every year, their brave stand is still commemorated by the Alport Castles Love Feast. Lud's Church, a secret chasm hidden in the trees of Back Forest north of the Roaches in the Staffordshire Moorlands, was used by fourteenth century Lollards for the same purpose, and is thought to take its name from one of their leaders, Walter de Ludank, whose daughter, Alice, was killed when soldiers raided a service. Lud's Church is also thought to have been the model for the Green Chapel in the classic early medieval alliterative poem, Sir Gawain and the Green Knight.

While it was non-Conformist Protestants who used Alport Castles Barn and Lud's Church to conduct their secret services, it was two Roman Catholic priests, Nicholas Garlick and Robert Ludlam, who were persecuted at Padley Chapel, near Grindleford, in the sixteenth century. They were taken in a raid on the chapel of Padley Hall, home of Sir Thomas Fitzherbert, and hanged, drawn and quartered at Derby for practicing their illegal religion in 1588. The Padley Martyrs are commemorated every July by a service at the chapel, which is all that now remains of the hall.

Opposite: The Castleton Garlanding King processes through the village under the shadow of Peveril Castle

THE 'LITTLE ROYAL SHOW'

Bakewell's two-day Agricultural Show held in the first week of August, is one of the biggest and best in the country, and attracts entries from all over the area and much further afield. It is known with some justification as 'the Little Royal Show'. Other agricultural shows are held at Hope and Ashbourne, while nationally-important sheepdog trials are held at Bamford, Dove Dale, Harden Moss, Hayfield, Hope and Longshaw. Competitors come to compete at these events from all over Britain, and the standards are extremely high.

CORN LAW RHYMER

Notable home-spun Peak District writers, apart from Hobbes, the philosopher who also published The Leviathan in 1651, and Cotton, are much harder to find. One of the earliest was Ebenezer Elliott (1781–1849), a master founder in Sheffield who became active in literature and politics, and was so incensed by the bread tax imposed on the poor that he composed a series of verses known as the Corn Law Rhymes *– thus attracting the nickname of the 'Corn Law Rhymer'. He came from Border Country stock, but was so well regarded in his adopted home that the workers of Sheffield paid for a bronze statue of him in Weston Park when he died.*

Customs such as rushbearing – strewing the floor with freshly-cut rushes – once common in all churches before the coming of carpets, are still retained in isolated churches such as at Macclesfield Forest Chapel, on the western edge of the National Park.

In predominately farming communities like the Peak District, events such as sheepdog trials, point-to-point horse races and local agricultural shows and markets, all have their parts to play in the rich tapestry of rural life. The weekly markets at Bakewell – now in the new Agricultural Centre – and Hope are important not only for the buying and selling of stock, but as social events where wives and neighbours can shop, meet and keep up with all the gossip of the dale.

LITERARY CONNECTIONS

The hills and dales of the Peak District have not spawned a William Wordsworth nor a William Shakespeare, although they have attracted a wide range of literary visitors and admirers over the years.

The first successful guidebook to the Peak District was probably Charles Cotton's *The Wonders of the Peake* first published in 1681. But this was merely a plagiarised and updated copy of Thomas Hobbes's *De Mirabilibus Pecci: Concerning the Wonders of the Peak in Darby-shire* published in 1636. In fact, the first mention of the Wonders of the Peak was by the Elizabethan historian, William Camden in 1586, who named nine of them in his *Britannia*.

This aping of the classical Seven Wonders of the Ancient World was a fashionable thing to do in the seventeenth century, and the 'Wonders' were: Peak Cavern at Castleton; Poole's Cavern and St Anne's Well at Buxton; Eldon Hole; the Ebbing and Flowing Well at Barmoor Clough; Mam Tor, and either Peak Forest or Chatsworth House, which was first promoted by Hobbes, who perhaps significantly was employed as a tutor by the Cavendish family.

Cotton combined with his friend, Izaak Walton, to produce the one true classic which has been written about the Peak District in the fisherman's bible, *The Compleat Angler*, first published in 1653 and third only to the Bible and the Book of Common Prayer as the most often reprinted book in English. In it, he praises the Dove as 'the princess of rivers' and the Lathkill as 'the purest and most transparent stream I ever yet saw, either at home or abroad'. And it bred, he added, 'the reddest and the best Trouts in England'.

One of the first travellers to record her impressions of the 'wilderness' of the Peak was Celia Fiennes, who is quoted at the start of this chapter. She was followed thirty years later on the Seven Wonders itinerary by Daniel Defoe, the cyncial journalist, political commentator and creator of *Robinson Crusoe* and *Moll Flanders*, on his *Tour Through the Whole Island of Great Britain*, in 1726.

Defoe poured scorn on Hobbes's and Cotton's Wonders, dismissing them all save Eldon Hole and Chatsworth, 'one a wonder of nature, the other of art'. He found the Peakrills 'a rude boorish kind of people' and the landscape to his eyes, was nothing more than 'a howling wilderness'.

But the age of the appreciation of the 'picturesque' and the Romantics was dawning, and later visitors like Lord Byron, who wrote that 'there are things in Derbyshire as noble as in Greece or Switzerland', and John Ruskin, who often visited Matlock as a child and called the county 'a lovely child's first alphabet; an alluring first lesson in all that is admirable', made the Peak District fashionable again.

It is widely believed that Jane Austen based parts of her famous novel *Pride and Prejudice* on the Peak District – and certainly parts of the recent television

adaptation were filmed at Lyme Park, near Stockport. It is thought that Jane visited Bakewell, staying at the newly-built Rutland Arms, in 1811, where she may have revised her novel. Thus Darcy's 'Pemberley' is supposed to be based on nearby Chatsworth (or maybe Willersley Castle at Cromford), and Bakewell is also featured as 'Lambton'.

Parts of the Hope Valley around Hathersage are also supposed to feature in Charlotte Brontë's novel *Jane Eyre* published in 1847. This was probably as a result of Charlotte's close friendship with Ellen Nussey, whose brother Henry, was the vicar of Hathersage. It is known that Charlotte visited Ellen and Henry at Hathersage in 1845 and stayed for three weeks. Several features in the novel, such as the name of the heroine and descriptions of the moors, seem to tie in with the Hathersage locality. Her description of Thornfield Hall – 'three stories high, of proportions not vast, though considerable: a gentleman's manor house, not a nobleman's seat: battlements round the top gave it a picturesque look' seems to match that of the fifteenth-century manor house of North Lees Hall – now a private guest house – above Hathersage precisely.

More recent authors of local note have been Robert Murray Gilchrist of Sheffield and Crichton Porteus, both of whom wrote about village life in the Peak District. G.H.B. Ward – the 'King of the Clarion Ramblers' of Sheffield – was the author of only one book, *The Truth about Spain*, which was published in 1913 and accurately forecast the Spanish Civil War. But his place in Peak District literary history is merited by those avidly-collected and marvellous examples of local historical research, the *Sheffield Clarion Handbooks*, which he almost single-handedly wrote and edited for fifty years.

The impressive entrance to Peak Cavern, Castleton – one of the traditional Wonders of the Peak and the largest cave entrance in Britain

6 Recreation

Opposite: Walkers emerge at the top of Jacob's Ladder on the realigned Pennine Way at the western end of Edale. This route has been extensively restored and reconstructed by the National Trust

The morning of Sunday, 24 April, 1932 dawned bright and sunny; the perfect day for ramblers from the surrounding industrial cities to get out and enjoy the unique sense of freedom offered by the beckoning Dark Peak moors.

But seventy years ago, that top-of-the-world feeling was available only to a privileged few, for most of the moorland of the Peak District was the strictly-private game reserve of a handful of wealthy owners. 'Trespassers will be Prosecuted' and 'Keep Out' signs dotted the access points to the moors, which were policed by heavy-handed and often abusive gamekeepers, employed to protect their masters' grouse from these hordes of invading townies.

At this time, only a dozen footpaths over 2 miles in length crossed 215 square miles (650sq km) of Peak District moorland, and not a single one crossed the 15 square miles (39sq km) of Kinder Scout – the highest point of the Peak and the natural magnet for hillwalkers. All that was about to change as a result of that bright Spring morning.

About 400 ramblers mainly from Manchester gathered on the picturesque cricket field of Hayfield, in the western shadow of Kinder Scout, intent on exercising what they believed to be their inalienable 'right to roam' across Kinder's boggy plateau. The event was organised by a Communist-inspired group known as the British Workers' Sports Federation which earlier that year had been turned off a ramble on Bleaklow by a band of threatening gamekeepers. Benny Rothman, secretary of the Lancashire branch of the group and others decided then and there that they would put the keepers to the test with a 'mass trespass', which was widely advertised.

So it was that the band of khaki-shorted ramblers set off, singing joyfully, up the Kinder Road, stopping at each stile until all were safely across. An impromptu speech by Rothman at the Bowden Bridge quarry, watched by painfully-obvious, dark-suited plain-clothed policemen, told them all why they were there. The historic spot, ironically now a car park used mainly by walkers, is marked by a bronze plaque set in the quarry face.

Then the happy band of ramblers set off for Kinder, walking up Nab Brow and into William Clough where, at a pre-arranged signal, they broke ranks and started to scramble up the forbidden slopes of Sandy Heys towards the plateau top. A line of about twenty keepers were waiting for them, and a few inconclusive scuffles took place, during which one keeper was slightly injured.

The ramblers held a 'victory meeting' near Ashop Head, and returned 'heads held high' to Hayfield, where the waiting police arrested six who were later charged with riotous assembly. Five, including Rothman, received prison sentences ranging from two and six months, and immediately became martyrs to the cause of free access.

The annual ramblers access demonstration in the Winnats Pass near Castleton a few weeks later attracted a huge crowd estimated at 10,000, and there were further organised trespasses on the Duke of Norfolk's Road at Abbey Brook in the

Top: An historic photograph which shows ramblers moving up Kinder Road, Hayfield at the start of the Mass Trespass on Kinder Scout on 24 April 1932. Taken nearly seventy years later the picture below shows the effect of millions of footsteps on the ridge from Mam Tor to Lose Hill. This section has now largely been paved with flagstones by the National Trust

A TASTE OF THE DARK PEAK

For a walk which gives a taste of the Dark Peak, try the ascent of Kinder by Crowden Brook, passing west through the weird gritstone tors of The Woolpacks to Noe Stool and Edale Cross, descending by the reconstructed Pennine Way via Jacob's Ladder to Edale. Less strenuous is the promenade along the Eastern Edges, from Froggatt or Curbar, returning by the banks of the River Derwent, or an even gentler stroll across the mini Dark Peak landscape and fascinating prehistoric landscape of Stanton Moor, near Bakewell.

Opposite: (top) The glorious summer promenade along the top of Froggatt Edge, with Bamford Edge and the Upper Derwent Moors beyond; (below) the reconstructed path through Dovedale, with the beetling limestone crag of Ravenstor in shadow on the right. This is one of the most heavily used footpaths in the National Park and an extensive programme of restoration is in progress

Overleaf: The sun lights Stanage Edge, one of the most famous climbing crags in the country, seen from across the valley of the Hood Brook, near Hathersage. Stanage has over 500 routes up its short, sharp gritstone faces

Upper Derwent, and on Stanage Edge. The harsh sentences inflicted on the Kinder trespassers had united the ramblers' cause, and acted as a significant catalyst towards eventual access to the countryside and National Park legislation.

When Sir Arthur Hobhouse made his recommendations for National Park status for the Peak two years after John Dower's seminal 1945 report, he commented: 'The controversy over access to uncultivated land reaches its height in the Peak, where landowners may draw their most remunerative rents from the lease of grouse moors, and where at the same time large areas are sterilized for water catchment. Many of the finest moorlands, where thousands wish to wander, are closed against 'trespassers' and an altercation with a gamekeeper may often mar a day's serenity. A national park in the Peak District will not justify its name unless this problem is satisfactorily solved.'

So when the Peak District National Park came into existence in April, 1951, one of the first jobs it did was to use the powers given it in the 1949 National Parks and Access to the Countryside Act to create access agreements with the owners of these once-forbidden moorlands, including Kinder Scout, Bleaklow and Black Hill. An indication of the importance placed on this work is that at one time, 60 per cent of all access agreements in Britain were to be found in the Peak District National Park, and they still cover over 80 square miles.

Walking and climbing are still the major recreational activities in the Peak, and as long ago as 1966, Eric Byne and Geoffrey Sutton could state in *High Peak*, their definitive history of walking and climbing in the area: 'Today more people walk and climb in the Peak than in all the other hills of Britain put together.' The same is probably true today; the central position and accessibility of the Peak means that it offers the nearest hill country and rock for climbing in a day trip to half the population of the country. And that ease of accessibility, as we shall see, brings its own problems in its wake.

WALKING

One of the main reasons for the enduring popularity of the Peak District among generations of walkers is the fact that it offers an unrivalled variety of walking opportunities in a relatively small area. If like those early trespassers you crave the wide open spaces and sense of freedom which only the open moors can provide, then the bleak and sometimes forbidding Dark Peak is the place for you. It also offers some of the toughest and roughest walking in Britain, because the fickle weather and notorious cloying, sticky peat bogs of Kinder, Bleaklow and Black Hill can sap the stamina of even the hardiest and fittest walker. The early 'bogtrotters' could skip across this difficult country at unbelieveable speed, and some of the classic walks, such as the 25-mile Marsden-Edale and 40-mile Derwent Watershed, were deliberately attempted in winter, when frost and snow at least gave the peat hags and groughs some kind of temporary stability.

One of Tom Stephenson's main reasons for his thirty-year battle to establish the 270-mile (435-km) Pennine Way – Britain's first and toughest National Trail – was to force the opening up of the Peak District and South Pennine Moors to walkers. Today, the Pennine Way is probably the best-known and certainly one of the heaviest-used footpaths in Britain. As it passes over the deep peat moors of Kinder Scout and Bleakow on the first stage of its journey north from Edale, long sections are now paved in an attempt to control and limit erosion by the thousands of pairs of boots which use it every year. The same treatment has had to be been given to other popular summits, such as Mam Tor, the Great Ridge to Lose

WHITE PEAK WALKING

One of the best and most popular dales walks is the 4-mile concessionary path through the National Nature Reserve of Lathkill Dale, starting either from Over Haddon or Monyash, returning by field paths above the dale. There is something of interest here for the observant walker at any time of the year. Another favourite walk is the circular walk from Alstonefield down into the Manifold Valley past Thor's Cave, north to Wettonmill or Ecton, and then back to Alstonefield. Or you could try linking the Tissington and High Peak Trails at Parsley Hay by walking down one and getting back to your starting place by the other by the use of one of the many stone-walled green lanes which cross the White Peak plateau.

For those not confident about route-finding or who want to learn a little more about the landscape through which they are walking, the Park Authority runs an extensive annual programme of guided walks organised by the Ranger Service during the summer months. Walking holidays are also run by the Losehill Hall Study Centre and others.

Opposite: (top) Climbers finish a climb on Stanage Edge – a mecca for rock climbers; (below) the Tissington Trail, formerly the Buxton–Ashbourne Railway line, is an easy, convenient and traffic-free route through some of the best of White Peak scenery and ideal for cyclists

Hill, Shutlingsloe and along Derwent Edge. The National Park Authority and the National Trust now employ full-time teams of path maintenance experts in order to cope with this ever-increasing army of walkers.

And it's not a problem which is confined to the Dark Peak moors, either. One of the most popular footpaths in the White Peak is the 7-mile route through Dovedale from the Stepping Stones to Hartington. This is the subject of a rolling programme of repair and maintenance by the authorities, so that when one section is complete and funds allow, it's time to move on to the next. The result is an all-weather footpath which can now be walked dryshod at any time of the year, and it has opened-up this most famous of the dales to a new constituency of less able or well equipped walkers who can now walk there safely and without too much trouble. Special stiles have been provided and other obstacles which the average walker takes for granted, have been removed.

The National Park Authority has an enlightened attitude towards disabled or less able visitors, and provisions such as a special Access for All booklet, the Ranger Service's Gateways Project and special facilities at places like Fairholmes in the Upper Derwent are making the Park more accessible to less active visitors. The prime examples of this are probably the famous railway trails, such as the Tissington and High Peak Trails, the Manifold Track and the Monsal Trail. These converted railway tracks, passing through some of the finest scenery of the White Peak, have been restored as walking, cycling or riding routes, and are eminently suitable for pushchairs or wheelchairs.

White Peak walking is quite different from that of its counterpart in the Dark Peak. Generally speaking it is less strenuous, although there are longer routes such as the 26-mile (42-km) White Peak Way from Matlock to Castleton. Walking through the dales is one of the most pleasant and popular types of walking in the Peak because Peak District dales, unlike those in Yorkshire, are generally too narrow to accommodate a road, so the only way to explore them is on foot.

CLIMBING

As well as being the birthplace and cockpit of the walking access movement, the Peak can also lay claim to being the birthplace of modern rock-climbing. Pioneering cragsmen like the Sheffield master cutler J.W.Puttrell were scaling Peak District crags as early as the 1890s, and they were soon joined by other middle and upper class tyros training for summer seasons in the Alps. Among these was the American vice-consul in Sheffield, Rice Kemper Evans, who explored many new routes at Stanage in the 1920s. But the greatest explosion in Peak District – and British – climbing came in the 1950s with the so-called 'working-class revolution'. Led by Manchester-born plumbers, Joe Brown and Don Whillans, both members of the newly-formed Rock and Ice Club, these tough and fearless young tradesmen led routes of ever-increasing severity with the minimum of equipment in places like The Roaches, Froggatt and Stanage Edges.

The cracks and fissures and rough, abrasive nature of Peak District gritstone were the perfect medium for the bold jamming techniques invented by climbers like Brown and Whillans, and they pushed forward the frontiers of the sport to new, previously unknown limits. It is no exaggeration to say that the modern sport of rock climbing was born here on the edges of Stanage, Froggatt and others.

Ignored by the early climbers as being too loose and dangerous, the steep and at times overhanging walls of limestone which marked the dales sides of the White Peak caught the attention of climbers in the 1960s and 1970s. Improved techniques and better equipment meant that these previously ignored faces could now be explored and routes of unheard of severity were soon being put up. Ravenstor, Water-cum-Jolly and Chee Tor in the valley of the Wye, along with High Tor at Matlock just outside the Park, became the new frontiers of the sport, and again the Peak was in the vanguard, where it remains to this day.

CAVING

Those earliest pioneer climbers like Puttrell were equally at home underground, exploring the many caves and fissures which are usually found where the limestone of the White Peak meets the shales and grit of the Dark, especially around Castleton. Although it does not have the wealth of potholes which are such a distinctive feature of the Carboniferous limestone of the Yorkshire Dales, the Peak nonetheless has an extensive caving tradition, and at places like Gautries Hole, Giant's Hole and P8 in the dry valley beneath Rushup Edge, some of the longest and deepest cave systems in Britain have been found. There are other systems in Stoney Middleton Dale, many of which, like so many other Peak District caves, were originally discovered by 't'owd man' – the lead miners who explored every available crevice for the valuable mineral. Many modern showcaves, such as Treak Cliff and Speedwell Mine at Castleton and Bagshaw Cavern at Bradwell, were also discovered in this way.

Eldon Hole, one of the original Seven Wonders of the Peak south of quarry-scarred Eldon Hill, is the largest open pot hole in the Peak but disappointingly despite its gaping void, it does not lead to an extensive system.

RIDING AND CYCLING

The earliest photographs of cyclists in the Peak District show crinoline-clad ladies in large hats daintily tripping over Dovedale's famous Stepping Stones, their bicycles resting on the bank. Despite the hills, the Peak District is a fine place to explore on bike, and the emergence of the all-terrain mountain bike has opened up even more areas through the network of bridleways which cross the Park. Many of these were originally used by the packhorses which were the long-distance juggernauts of their day, and some are still paved with the original stones which echoed to the clatter of the hooves of the Jaeger ponies.

The pony-trekking centre of the Peak District is at Edale, in the shadow of Kinder Scout. But there are many miles of pleasant routes, including the Tissington and High Peak Trails, which wind across the hills throughout the Park for those who enjoy their scenery from horseback.

Many visitors bring their own bikes to the National Park these days, and they can certainly extend the limits of your exploration while leaving the car behind. But even if the visitor does not own his or her own bike, the Park Authority and

Top: Yachting on the Torside Reservoir in Longdendale, in the north of the National Park. Torside is one of few reservoirs in the Park which have sailing clubs, where boats can be hired by non-members

Above: The Tissington Trail provides safe off-road riding for youngsters

others have provided a network of cycle hire centres in popular places such as on the traffic-free Tissington Trail and in the Upper Derwent Valley. Here you can hire a bike, including specially-adapted ones to carry young children or disabled people, for a few hours or an entire day depending on how much time you have. In another attempt to encourage visitors to leave their cars at home, the Park Authority has neogitated a deal with the railway company which allows you to bring your bike free of charge on the Hope Valley railway line.

WATERSPORTS

One thing that the Peak District lacks is any notable stretches of 'white water' which would attract canoeists, with the sole exception of the Derwent as it runs through Matlock and Matlock Bath. But there many other ways in which the plentiful water of the National Park can be enjoyed, most notably on some of the larger reservoirs.

There are thriving sailing clubs at Errwood Reservoir in the Goyt Valley and Torside Reservoir in Longdendale, from where daily or hourly tickets can be obtained for beginners or those without their own boats, whether they be sailing boats, canoes or kayaks. The only place where waterskiing is allowed is on Bottoms Reservoir, just outside the Park at the foot of Longdendale, where, as at Errwood, there are also facilities for the increasingly-popular sport of windsurfing.

AIR SPORTS

An increasingly-common sight soaring in the Peak District skies above places like Stanage Edge and Mam Tor are the colourful shapes of hang-gliders and parascenders. These bat-like aircraft offer a tremendous sense of freedom for those who partake in the sport, and also provide a wonderful spectator sport for those who are just content to watch from the ground. There are training schools in and around the Peak for those who want to try these ultimate 'up, up and away' sports, while no training is needed for another, hot-air ballooning.

Ballooning is one of the finest ways to view the varied Peak District landscape, as you float silently along where the prevailing wind takes you. A hot-air balloon is an excellent camera platform for the photographer, but the sport, which is operated by a number of specialist companies in the Peak District, is always obviously dependent on the right weather conditions.

The same conditions of rising thermals as they hit the Peak District hills is essential to the success of traditional gliding, which has been carried out from Hucklow Edge by the Derbyshire and Lancashire Gliding Club since 1935. This is one of the oldest gliding clubs in the country, with one of the most spectacular launch sites at 1,360ft (415m) above the sea at Camphill. Special training flights are always available, plus week or fortnight long gliding holidays, based at the club house which occupies a former farmhouse on the site.

COMPLETE ANGLING

Angling has a very long and distinguished history in the Peak District. In fact, it could be argued that it was the first sport to be recognised in the area, through Izaak Walton and Charles Cotton's The Compleat Angler, *first published in 1653 and still in print today. Walton and Cotton praised the clear, translucent and trout-bearing waters of the Dove, Wye and Lathkill and even today, they are much-prized by anglers who will pay large sums for a licence to fish them. Most of the fishing in Peak District rivers is private, although some hotels offer day or week licences for their guests. Day tickets for fishing for the brown and rainbow trout which are artifically stocked at Ladybower, Errwood and Combs Reservoirs are available from the appropriate water company.*

Opposite: Paragliding is an increasingly popular sport from places like Stanage Edge. Along with hang-gliding, it is also a popular spectactor sport, attracting many admirers from the ground

Exploring the Park

Above: (left) The River Lathkill runs through the pretty village of Alport, near Youlgreave; (right) a unique double inn sign crosses the main street in Ashbourne – the neat Georgian town often described as the 'Gateway to Dovedale'

ALPORT

There are two Alports in the Peak District; one is an isolated hamlet in the remote Alport Valley south of Bleaklow, famous for its spectacular landslip said to be the largest in Britain and known as Alport Castles. Better known is the charming village of Alport which stands at the confluence of the Lathkill and Bradford rivers, near Youlgreave. Its cottages mainly date from the seventeenth and eighteenth centuries, and its wealth was founded, like so many other White Peak villages, on lead mining.

ALSTONEFIELD

This stone-built Staffordshire village standing at 900ft (274m) on a ridge between the Dove and the Manifold is well-named. Surrounded by a network of drystone walls and at least two miles from the nearest main road, Alstonefield remains a typically-unspoilt White Peak village. It is watched over by the tower of its medieval church in which an elaborate pew is dedicated to the Cotton family of nearby, but now demolished, Beresford Hall in Dovedale. The George on the village green at Alstonefield is a famous and popular walkers' pub, which welcomes booted customers with good food and ale.

ASHBOURNE

Ashbourne is just outside the National Park boundary, but proclaims itself as 'the Gateway to Dovedale'. But there is much more to this charming, mainly Georgian town than that. The triangular, sloping Market Place where, in 1745, Bonnie Prince Charlie declared his father to be King James III, leads down to Church

Street, bridged by a unique double inn sign for the Green Man and Black's Head. Here are some of the finest Georgian houses in Derbyshire, including The Mansion, where Samuel Johnson was a regular guest. Further down Church Street is the mullioned and gabled Old Grammar School, which was founded in 1585 by Sir Thomas Cockayne on behalf of Queen Elizabeth I.

St Oswald's Parish Church, with its elegant 212ft (30m) spire, was described by the Victorian novelist George Eliot as 'the finest mere parish church in England', and it is certainly one of the most interesting. Don't miss the Cockayne and Bradbourne monuments in the north transept chapel, or Thomas Banks' s famous white marble monument to five-year-old Penelope Boothby.

Ashbourne is famous for its Shrovetide Football Game, a boisterous event played through the streets of the town between the 'Up'ards' and the 'Down'ards', and for its delicious gingerbread.

ASHFORD-IN-THE-WATER

Famous for its six well-dressings held in early June, Ashford is not exactly in-the-Water but on the River Wye, which is crossed by the much-photographed, medieval low-arched Sheepwash Bridge. Occasionaly, the bridge is still used for its original purpose, and large crowds still gather to watch the sheep being thrown into the Wye to get their fleeces clean before shearing.

Ashford's Parish Church was largely rebuilt in 1870, but it retains the base of its squat, thirteenth-century tower, and inside contains some fine examples of Ashford's most famous product, the polished limestone known as Ashford Black Marble.

Above: The Parish Church of the Holy Trinity, Ashford

Below: The medieval Sheepwash Bridge across the River Wye at Ashford-in-the-Water is still used for its ancient purpose once a year

BAKEWELL

With a population of 4,000, Bakewell is the largest town and natural capital of the Peak District National Park. The Park Authority has its headquarters here at Aldern House on Baslow Road, but these modern planners are following in the footsteps of an administrative history which goes back to Saxon times.

Evidence of this is provided by the two Saxon preaching crosses and other Saxon work in the restored hilltop parish church of All Saints. There are records of King Edward the Elder holding an important 'summit meeting' with other kings in the neighbourhood of Bakewell in 920AD. The Normans built a motte and bailey castle at the crossing of the Wye near the splendid Town Bridge, which dates from the thirteenth century and is still in constant use by modern traffic.

In the centre of town stands the Old Market Hall, an attractive, gabled seventeenth-century building which is now the town's National Park and Tourist Information Centre. The right to hold a market in Bakewell was first granted in 1254 and that right is still exercised every Monday in the controversially-modernistic Agricultural and Business Centre across the Wye from the town. Bakewell still acts as the main

Above: The Lower Courtyard of the Duke of Rutland's Haddon Hall, near Bakewell, slopes gently towards the river. The medieval perfection of Haddon sees it in frequent use as a ready-made set by film and television companies

Right: A winter view of Bakewell's splendid Town Bridge over the River Wye. Originally constructed in the early fourteenth century but widened in the nineteenth century it has carried heavy traffic into the market town for 700 years

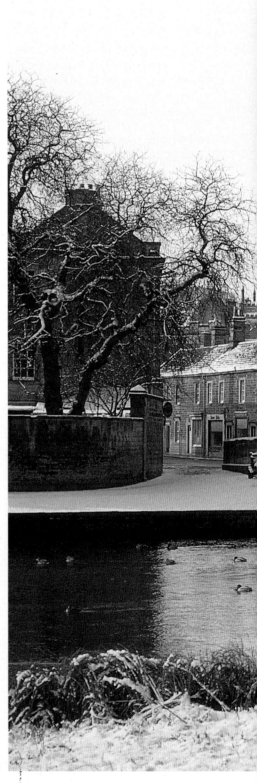

Opposite: The great dome of the Royal Devonshire Hospital at Buxton, once the largest unsupported dome in the world, viewed from The Slopes

livestock market for the entire Peak District, and every July, the Bakewell Agricultural Show is one of the biggest and best in the country.

Other important buildings in Bakewell include the Old House in Cunningham Place, behind the church, which is probably the oldest house in the town and now the home of the Bakewell Historical Society's excellent museum; and the early nineteenth century Rutland Arms, where the town's most famous export, the Bakewell pudding, was inadvertently invented after a mistake by the cook.

Just down the A6 towards Matlock is the romantic pile of medieval Haddon Hall, Derbyshire home of the Duke of Rutland.

BAMFORD

Bamford is a hillside village beneath Bamford Edge and on the road to the Ladybower and Upper Derwent dams. The dead from the drowned villages of Derwent and Ashopton were disinterred and buried in Bamford's parish church of St John the Baptist when the Ladybower Reservoir was built during the World War II. Bamford Mill on the Derwent was formerly a cotton mill built in 1820 and later made electrical furnaces. Today it has been converted for luxury housing. Bamford Sheepdog Trials, held on Spring Bank Holiday Monday, are among the best-attended and most famous in the Peak.

BASLOW

Baslow stands at the northern gates of Chatsworth, and the village's history is inextricably linked with the fortunes of the Cavendish family. For that reason, the major hotel in the village, one of the best in the Peak, is the Devonshire Arms.

At Nether End, near one of Baslow's two fine bridges over the Derwent, you can see one of the few remaining thatched cottages in the Park, and the parish church of St Anne's has an unusual clockface decorated with the legend VICTORIA 1897 instead of numbers, to commemorate the Queen's jubilee in that year.

The elegant fifteenth-century bridge across the River Derwent is built on the site of a former ford. A tiny watchman's shelter still exists on the village (eastern) side.

Top: The bridge across the River Derwent at Bridge End, Baslow
Above: Climbers silhouetted against the skyline on Robin Hood's Stride near Birchover

BIRCHOVER

Birchover marches up from the weird oucrop of Rowtor Rock behind the celebrated Druid's Inn to the heather covered heights of Stanton Moor, where local father and son team J.C. and J.P. Heathcote excavated over seventy Bronze Age burial mounds. They housed their collection of finds in the old village post office and it is now in the Weston Park Museum in Sheffield.

Tiny Rowtor Chapel, below the rocks and the Druid Inn (famous for its food), was restored by Thomas Eyre and features fragments of Norman work and some strange carvings and decorations. Nearby across the fields are two other strange gritstone outcrops, known as Cratcliff Tor and Robin Hood's Stride. The latter also had the nickname of Mock Beggar's Hall from its resemblance to a ruined mansion.

BRADFIELD, HIGH AND LOW

The two Bradfields occupy the top and bottom of the Loxley Valley, which bites deep into the north-eastern moors of the Peak District. Low Bradfield clusters around its lovely cricket ground, while High Bradfield, the bigger of the two, is centred on the magnificent parish church of St Nicholas, which commands one of the finest views from any Peak District church, over the Damflask and Agden Reservoirs. The church dates mainly from the late fifteenth century but has a fine, fourteenth century tower and in a corner of the churchyard, boasts a rare Watch House, where observation was kept to repel body-snatchers in the eighteenth century. In the fields nearby are the remains of two Norman motte and bailey castles, reflecting the former importance of this now peaceful South Yorkshire village.

BRADWELL

'Bradder' as this Hope Valley village is known locally, has a long and chequered history. It starts with the Romans, and the finest remains of that period to be found in the National Park are at Brough a mile north of the village where the small fortlet of *Navio* was situated above a bend in the River Noe.

Later, after the Romans had departed, the mysterious earthwork known as the Grey Ditch was constructed north of the village. During the Middle Ages and later, Bradwell was an important centre for lead mining, and the distinctive miner's hats, known as 'Bradder beavers' were made here. Bagshawe Cavern, now open to visitors for adventure caving trips, was accidentally discovered by lead miners in 1806.

Bradwell was also the birthplace of Samuel Fox, the inventor of the folding-frame umbrella, and other village industries have included cotton goods, telescopes and spectacles. It holds its well-dressings during August.

BUXTON

The reason why Buxton was excluded from the National Park becomes obvious as you approach it from the south on the A6. As you drop off the limestone plateau, enormous quarry faces open up on your right at Tunstead. Buxton in fact is almost ringed by gigantic quarries, so the Park boundary was drawn neatly around it.

Despite its industrial setting, Buxton retains the slightly faded air of a spa town, and during the eighteenth century, the 5th Duke of Devonshire expended large sums of money in a vain attempt to make it a rival to Bath and Cheltenham. It was during this period that the grand and recently restored Crescent was built to a design by John Carr; and the Natural Baths and the Great Stables – now the Royal Devonshire Hospital – were also constructed at this boom time for the spa town. Later came the grand hilltop Town Hall above the planned gardens of The Slopes, the imposing Palace Hotel which came with the opening of the Midland railway, and the mock-baroque Opera House, built by Frank Matcham in 1905. This ornate building is now the home of the annual international Buxton Festival of Music and the Arts.

It was the Romans who first discovered the health-giving properties of its warm (28°C) springs and named the town *Aquae Arnemetiae* – 'the spa of the goddess of the grove'. St Anne's Well, opposite The Crescent, still provides that health-giving elixir freely to passers-by. Earlier residents may have used Poole's Cavern in Green Lane, where prehistoric remains have been found in what is now a show cavern.

CASTLETON

Castleton, as its name suggests, is the town of the castle – in this case William Peveril's imposing curtain wall and keep which still lords it over the gridiron plan

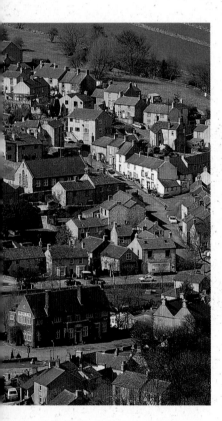

A view across the rooftops of the busy little village of Bradwell in the Hope Valley from Bradwell Edge. Famous for its ice-cream, Bradwell was founded on the wealth of lead mining

of the medieval township beneath. The site was granted to Peveril by William the Conqueror in order to administer the king's lead mining and hunting interests, at the centre of the Royal Forest of the Peak. The spectacular site of the castle on a rocky spur between the Peak Cavern gorge and Cave Dale is one of the most impressive in Britain and is now in the care of English Heritage.

Beneath the walls of the castle, the fame of modern Castleton is based fairly and squarely on tourism, with its four show caves attracting thousands of visitors annually. The oldest of these is Peak Cavern, said to have the largest cave entrance in Britain which was once the home of a community of rope-makers; Treak Cliff on the now-closed road which leads towards the hillfort-topped, 'Shivering Mountain' of Mam Tor; Blue John directly beneath Mam Tor and named after the semi-precious variety of fluorspar found only here, and Speedwell Cavern, found

The medieval township of Castleton, as seen from above Cave Dale, with the Great Ridge leading to Lose Hill in the background. The originally Norman parish church of St Edmund is in the centre of the picture

Opposite: The spire of the parish church of St Peter at Edensor peeps out through the mist in this autumn view across the Derwent Valley from Gardom's Edge

by lead miners and reached by an underground canal. Speedwell stands at the foot of the craggy gorge of the Winnats Pass, which now takes the main road again after the final collapse of the Mam Tor road in the 1970s.

Castleton is the scene each Oak Apple Day (29 May) of a unique and probably originally pagan ceremony known as the Garlanding. A rider known as the King is encased in a beehive-shaped structure covered in flowers, and rides around the town with his Queen to a tune not unlike the Cornish Floral Dance. The garland is then hoisted to the top of the tower of the parish church of St Edmund and left to wither and die, in what is thought to be a welcome for Spring.

CHELMORTON

The one-street village of Chelmorton is one of the highest in the Peak, watched over by the twin tumulus-topped height of Chelmorton Low (1,463ft/446m). It is famous among landscape historians for its perfectly-preserved pattern of strip fields running back on either side of the village street, down which runs the delightfully-named Illy Willy Water. These ancient medieval fields have been 'fossilised' by eighteenth-century enclosure walls, and many are now protected by the National Park Authority. The parish church of St John the Baptist is topped by a locust weathervane – in commemoration of the Baptist's time spent in the wilderness.

CRESSBROOK

Cressbrook is best known for its magnificent Cressbrook Mill, one of the best remaining examples of a Georgian cotton mill in Britain. Beautifully situated in the deep valley of the River Wye where it is joined by Ravensdale, the original mill at Cressbrook was built by Richard Arkwright, but burned down in 1785. The present pedimented and cupola-topped building was erected in 1815, but is a sad sight today as yet another of the Peak's magnificent heritage of cotton mills seeking a new use.

William Newton, the so-called 'Minstrel of the Peak', was manager at the mill and was said to have been a model employer, unlike Ellis Needham at Litton Mill, just upstream, whose inhumane treatment of his apprentices became a *cause célèbre* in the early nineteenth century.

EDALE

The village now known as Edale, famous as the start of the Pennine Way, is more properly named Grindsbrook Booth. Edale is the name of the valley of the River Noe which drains the southern slopes of Kinder Scout, at 2,088ft (636m), the highest point in the National Park. The five hamlets which punctuate its length are all called 'booths', an old word meaning a temporary shelter for herdsmen. The five Edale booths are, from the east, Nether Booth, Ollerbrook Booth, Grindsbrook Booth, Barber Booth and Upper Booth, but Grindsbrook Booth takes priority purely because it is the largest settlement. It is also a railway station on the so-called 'Ramblers' Route' between Sheffield and Stockport, and the National Park's Visitor and Ranger Centre at Fieldhead, so forming the natural focus for the valley.

Top: 'Fossilised' medieval strip fields at Chelmorton. This is one of the classic sites for this type of land use in Britain
Above: The Old Nag's Head (right) at Edale – the start of the Pennine Way – with the crags of the southern edge of Kinder Scout beyond

The 300-year-old Nag's Head Inn is the traditional start of the 270-mile (435-km) Pennine Way National Trail, which winds up the watershed of England to Kirk Yetholm, across the Scottish border.

EDENSOR

Pronounced 'Ensor', this pretty estate village lies in the parklands of Chatsworth, and was built in 1839 by the 6th Duke of Devonshire, apparently because the

original village was deemed too close to the house and spoiled the view. An eccentric, though somehow pleasing, mixture of architectural styles characterises the village, with the graceful spire of Sir George Gilbert Scott's parish church dominating the scene.

EYAM

Eyam (pronounced 'Eem') cannot escape its age-old epithet of 'the Plague Village', although recent research has questioned whether it really was the plague which decimated the village population in the years 1665–66. Whatever the diagnosis, the heroic action of the villagers in imposing a quarantine on their movements to stop the disease spreading cannot be denied, and there are touching memorials on several cottages commemorating those who died during the frightful 'visitation'.

There is a Plague Book in the parish church of St Lawrence which gives the names of the 350 victims, along with vicar William Mompesson's chair and other relicts. Mompesson's wife, Catherine, was one of the victims and is buried in the churchyard near the venerable truncated Saxon preaching cross, a masterpeice of Celtic craftsmanship. More touching memorials are to be found in the fields surrounding the village, such as the Riley Graves where a mother buried her whole family, and the Eyam Museum in Hawkhill Road also tells the story of the plague.

The annual plague commemoration service is held to coincide with the well-dressings in late August at Cucklett Delph, a limestone crag near the village where services where held in the open air during the visitation. Eyam Hall, the charming home of the Wright family for over three centuries, was built shortly after the plague episode, and is now open to the public.

GREAT HUCKLOW

This former lead mining village sits below Hucklow Edge, where the gliders from the Derbyshire and Lancashire Gliding Club soar effortlessly from their site at Camphill on every suitable day. The club was founded in 1935 as one of the earliest in the country, and its launching site at over 1,360ft (415m) above the Hope Valley must be one of the most spectacular. Just along the ridge from the gliding club site is the Barrel Inn, dating from 1637 and one of the oldest in Derbyshire. Great Hucklow, a workaday village today, was formerly famous for its Hucklow Players, a talented group of amateur dramatists led by author and broadcaster Laurence du Garde Peach. The plays were performed in a Unitarian holiday home and attracted audiences from all over Britain.

GREAT LONGSTONE

The name of the village inn, the Crispin, gives away the nature of one of Longstone's traditional trades, that of boot-making. This one-street village has some good eighteenth- and nineteenth-century houses, notably Longstone Hall (private) built in 1747, and its wealth was founded, like so many White Peak villages, on lead mining. Nearby Longstone Edge is now being quarried for fluorspar, the mineral lead miners threw away as waste.

Top: The stocks on the village green at Eyam, with seventeenth-century Eyam Hall beyond. Eyam Hall, recently opened to the public, has been in the Wright family for 300 years

Above: The intricately carved Saxon preaching cross in Eyam churchyard

GRINDLEFORD

Grindleford is strung out for 2 miles along the River Derwent, which is crossed by a fine, three-arched bridge. It gets its name from the grindstones which were quarried from nearby Froggatt and Curbar Edges for many years. Nearby is Padley Gorge (National Trust) one of the best examples of a semi-natural sessile oak woodland in the National Park, and the summer home for a famous colony of pied flycatchers. Padley Chapel is all that remains of the manor house of Padley Hall, from where two Catholic priests were taken to be hanged, drawn and quartered at the height of the Reformation in 1588.

HARTINGTON

The spacious square of Hartington, at the northern end of Dovedale, shows that it was once an important market centre, and in fact was granted the right as early as 1203. The hilltop parish church of St Giles reflects this early importance and stands at the centre of one of the biggest parishes in the country.

Today, Hartington is a tourist village popular with walkers, and perhaps most famous for its cheese factory, which is one of a handful in the country which is allowed to make the blue-veined Stilton – 'the King of English Cheeses'.

The Burbage Brook runs through the autumn splendour of Padley Gorge, near Grindleford, one of the finest semi-natural oak woodlands in the National Park

HATHERSAGE

The fictional home of Little John, loyal friend of Robin Hood, Hathersage is a prosperous Hope Valley village which spreads comfortably beneath the popular gritstone climbing crags of Stanage Edge. Once the centre of a thriving needle and pin-making industry, Hathersage was also a centre for the making of grind and millstones, quarried from the nearby gritstone edges where many abandoned examples are still to be found.

The parish church of St Michael has some of the finest memorial brasses in the Peak, mainly to the powerful local Eyre family, who built the commanding Tudor tower house of North Lees Hall east of the village.

HAYFIELD

Beneath the western slopes of Kinder Scout, Hayfield was formerly a centre of industry, with woollen, cotton, papermaking and textile printing mills using the power from the rivers Sett and Kinder. Today is it probably best-known as a walking centre, and was the scene in 1932 for the starting point of the famous Kinder Scout Mass Trespass, which highlighted the lack of access to some of the Peak's highest and wildest moorlands. The mainly Georgian parish church of St Matthew, close to the river bridge, was the scene of two alleged 'resurrections' in the eighteenth century.

HOPE

This bustling village on the A625 once was the centre of a parish which covered two-thirds of the Royal Forest of the Peak, and there are reminders of its former importance in the parish church of St Peter. It was also important enough to give

Judging a sheep class at the annual Hope Show, held in the tiny village which gave the valley its name and which still has a weekly livestock market

its name to the whole of the Hope Valley, and still hosts a twice-weekly agricultural market and the Hope Agricultural Show in August.

ILAM

The neat, pretty estate village of Ilam stands at the confluence of the Dove and Manifold valleys, just inside Staffordshire. It was the shipping magnate Jesse Watts Russell who rebuilt Ilam Hall (now a National Trust property and Youth Hostel) in a battlemented Gothic style and redesigned the village, installing the imitation Eleanor Cross at its centre in memory of his first wife. The saddleback-towered parish church has an interesting shrine to the Saxon St Bertram and Saxon crosses in the churchyard.

LONGNOR

This moorland township on a ridge between the Upper Dove and Manifold Valleys has a cobbled Market Square with a Market Hall complete with tolls and charges, now used as a craft centre. Longnor is a convenient centre for exploring the less-frequented upper reaches of the Dove and Manifold, with their distinctive reef limestone peaks.

A distant view of Longnor, the former market town in the Staffordshire moorlands, built on a ridge between the Dove and the Manifold

MATLOCK AND MATLOCK BATH

The Matlocks are just outside the National Park boundary, but the southern entrance to the Peak District for most visitors. Matlock's fame was founded on John Smedley's Hydro – now Derbyshire's County Hall – but the earlier village, known as Old Matlock, was centred to the east around the parish church.

Matlock Bath is a mile to the south, filling the bottom of the impressive Derwent Gorge and watched over by the imposing 300ft (90m) crag of High Tor. There are show caves on the Heights of Abraham on the opposite banks, where cable cars take visitors to the Victoria Tower which marks the summit. The Peak District Mining Museum in the Pavilion is a must for those interested in the history of Peak District lead mining.

MONYASH

Monyash, high on the White Peak plateau at the head of Lathkill Dale, was the site of one of the Barmote Courts which administered lead mining during the eighteenth and nineteenth centuries. Grouped around its ancient market cross on the village green, Monyash is a typical nucleated village probably founded because of its 'meres' or ponds which were so vital on the fast-draining limestone. It was once a centre for the Quaker movement, and John Gratton, a prominent preacher, lived at One Ash Grange.

PEAK FOREST

Named after the medieval Royal Forest of the Peak, Peak Forest is high on the limestone plateau and despite the name doesn't boast many trees. The interesting parish church, unusually dedicated to King Charles the Martyr, became known as 'the Gretna Green of the Peak' because of a quirk of eccesiastical law. Nearby, on the slopes of Eldon Hill, is Eldon Hole, the biggest natural pothole in the Peak and one of the original Seven Wonders.

Monyash is a typical White Peak village, high on the limestone plateau

STANTON-IN-THE-PEAK

Stanton is a hillside village which climbs up the western flank of Stanton Moor, one of the richest prehistoric sites in the Peak. Over seventy Bronze Age burial mounds have been discovered under the heather, but the most important site is the Nine Ladies Stone Circle, sheltered in a birchwood clearing. Stanton is the estate village for the Thornhills, who still live at Stanton Hall.

STONEY MIDDLETON

Stoney Middleton shelters in the depths of Middleton Dale, which is despoiled by limestone quarries at its western end. Midway between the Roman forts of Navio (Brough) and Chesterfield, there are strong local claims for Roman settlement, but there is no evidence despite the name of the recently-restored Roman Baths in The Nook. Nearby is the odd octagonally-shaped parish church of St Martin.

TIDESWELL

Tideswell is a large village of ancient foundation, as witnessed by its magnificent parish church of St John the Baptist, often dubbed 'the Cathedral of the Peak'. The church was built in the Decorated style in only seventy years at the height of Tideswell's fortune during the Middle Ages. The Perpendicular tower was added

The parish church of St John the Baptist at Tideswell, often referred to as 'the Cathedral of the Peak'

Above: The pretty Fitzherbert estate village of Tissington as seen from across its village pond or mere. Tissington is the scene of the first Peak District well dressings, held on Ascension Day each year

Opposite: (top) A colourful well dressing at Youlgreave, which boasts some of the finest examples of this unique form of folk art in the National Park; (below) the seventeenth-century Market Hall in Winster, which became the first property acquired by the National Trust in the Peak District in 1906. The redbrick building was once open at ground floor level, where the trading took place

later but the whole creates a wonderful uniformity of style and appearance. There are some fine monuments and brasses, especially the one to Bishop Robert Purseglove, one of Tideswell's greatest sons and benefactors, who died in 1579.

Tideswell's famous well dressings take place during Wakes Week in June.

TISSINGTON

The 'modern' tradition of well-dressing is said to have been started at Tissington in 1350, when the villagers wanted to give thanks for the fact that their pure springs had saved them from the ravages of the Black Death of 1348-49. But it is almost certain that the tradition goes back much further than that, to pagan times when the life-giving gift of water was so important to communities like this. Today, Tissington's well-dressing are still the earliest, from Ascension Day, and among the best. Five wells or springs are decorated, and attract huge crowds of visitors.

Tissington is another pretty little estate village, this time owned by the Fitzherberts who still live at Tudor Tissington Hall, recently opened to the public. The squat tower of St Mary's parish church reveals its Norman origins.

WINSTER

A beautifully complete eighteenth-century village centred on its seventeenth-century arched Market Hall (National Trust). Winster was another lead mining village, and there are many remains of 't'owd man' in the surrounding fields, including a restored Ore House near the Miners' Arms on the hill above the village. The Winster Morris Men are one of the oldest troupes in the country, and have their own dance and tune.

YOULGREAVE

Over sixty variations have been recorded of the name of this busy, one-street village on the hill above Bradford Dale. The name is thought to mean 'the yellow grove' or 'Geola's grove' – a groove being the old name for a lead mine – and Youlgreave was certainly at the centre of this once-importance industry. Youlgreave's parish church of All Saints is one of the finest in the Peak District, and its fine, pinnacled Perpendicular tower dominates the village. There are fine monuments inside to the Cockayne and Gylbert families.

Youlgreave's famous well-dressings date only from 1829 when the strange circular Fountain in the centre of the village was set up as the storage tank for the village's own water supply, which it still enjoys. Among Youlgreave's interesting buildings are the seventeenth-century Old Hall and the Youth Hostel, which was formerly the village Co-operative Society store.

Information

USEFUL ADDRESSES

Peak District National Park Authority
Aldern House
Baslow Road
Bakewell
Derbyshire DE45 1AE
Tel: 01629 816200

National Trust – East Midland Region
Stable Courtyard
Clumber Park
Worksop
Nottinghamshire S80 3BE
Tel: 01909 486411

National Park Information Centres

Bakewell Information Centre
Old Market Hall
Bridge Street
Bakewell
Tel: 01629 813227

Castleton Information Centre
Castle Street
Castleton

Hope Valley
Derbyshire
Tel: 01433 620679

Edale Information Centre
Fieldhead
Edale
Hope Valley
Tel: 01433 870207

Fairholmes Information Centre
Upper Derwent Valley
Tel: 01433 650953
Torside Information Centre
Longdendale (no phone)

Other bodies

English Nature – Peak District Team
Manor Barn
Over Haddon
Bakewell
Derbyshire DE45 1JE
Tel: 01629 815095

English Heritage – East Midlands
Hazelrigg House
33 Marefair

Northampton NN1 1SR
Tel: 01604 730350

Heart of England Tourist Board
Premier House
15 Wheeler Gate
Nottingham NG1 2NA
Tel: 0115 959 8383

Forestry Commission
Rydal House
Colton Road
Rugeley
Staffordshire WS15 3HF
01889 585222

Derbyshire Wildlife Trust
Elvaston Castle
Derby
Derbyshire DE72 3EP
Tel: 01332 756610

Staffordshire Wildlife Trust
Coutts House
Sandon
Stafford ST18 0DN
Tel: 01889 508534

Left: The Moat Stone: one of the unusual tors on the southern edge of Kinder Scout
Overleaf: The Trinnacle overlooks the valley of the Greenfield Brook in the north-west of the Park

Maps

The use of the excellent appropriate Ordnance Survey maps is highly recommended for any detailed exploration of the National Park, espeecially if you are leaving the car behind and venturing out into the countryside.

Outdoor Leisure Maps (1:25,000) No 1 Peak District – Dark Peak; No 24 Peak District – White Peak Landrangers (1:50,000) No 110 Sheffield & Huddersfield; No 119 Buxton, Matlock and Dovedale

Attractions

Chatsworth House
Bakewell
Derbyshire DE45 1PP
Tel: 01246 582204

Haddon Hall
Bakewell
Derbyshire DE45 1LA
Tel: 01629 812855

Lyme Park
Disley
Stockport, Cheshire SK12 2NX
Tel: 01663 762023

Eyam Hall
Eyam
Hope Valley
Derbyshire S32 5QW
Tel: 01433 631976

Peveril Castle
Castleton
Hope Valley
Derbyshire S33 8WQ
Tel: 01433 620613

Peak District Mining Museum
The Pavilion

Matlock Bath
Derbyshire DE4 3NR
Tel: 01629 583834

Peak Cavern
Castleton
Hope Valley
Derbyshire S33 8WS
Tel: 01433 620285

Blue John Cavern
Castleton
Hope Valley
Derbyshire S33 8WP
Tel: 01433 620638

Speedwell Cavern
Winnats Pass
Castleton
Hope Valley
Derbyshire S33 8WP
Tel: 01433 620512

Treak Cliff Cavern
Castleton
Hope Valley
Derbyshire S33 8WA
Tel: 01433 620571

Tissington Hall
Tissington
Ashbourne
Derbyshire DE6 1RA
Tel: 01335 390246

Caudwell's Mill and Craft Centre
Rowsley
Matlock
Derbyshire DE4 2EB
Tel: 01629 734374

Eyam Museum
Hawkhill Road
Eyam
Hope Valley
Derbyshire S32 5QP
Tel: 01433 631371

Castleton Village Museum
Methodist Church Schoolroom
Buxton Road
Castleton
Derbyshire S33 8WP
Tel: 01433 620950

FURTHER READING

Anderson, P., and Shimwell, D. *Wild Flowers and other Plants of the Peak District* (Moorland, 1981)

Barnatt, John, and Smith, Ken. *Peak District – Landscapes through Time* (Batsford/English Heritage, 1997)

Byne, Eric, and Sutton, Geoffrey. *High Peak* (Secker and Warburg, 1966)

Dodd, A.E. and E.M. *Peakland Roads and Trackways* (Moorland, 1974)

Edwards, K.C. *The Peak District* (Collins New Naturalist, 1962)

Ford, Trevor D. *The Story of Peak District Rocks and Scenery* (National Trust, no date)

Ford, Trevor D., and Rieuwerts, J.H. ed. *Lead Mining in the Peak District* (Peak Park Joint Planning Board, 1968)

Frost, R.A. *Birds of Derbyshire* (Moorland, 1978)

Harris, Helen. *Industrial Archaeology of the Peak District* (David & Charles, 1971)

Hodges, Richard. *Wall to Wall History* (Duckworth, 1991)

Millward, Roy, and Robinson, Adrian. *The Peak District* (Eyre Methuen, 1975)

Smith, Roland. *First and Last* (Peak Park Joint Planning Board, 1978)

Smith, Roland. *Peak National Park* (Webb & Bower/Michael Joseph, 1987)

Various authors. *Peak District Leisure Guide* (AA/Ordnance Survey, 1987)

Wolverson Cope, F. *Geology Explained in the Peak District* (David & Charles, 1976)

Index

Page numbers in *italics* indicate illustrations